The HOPE *of* GLORY

A Preview of Things to Come

WARREN HENDERSON

The Hope of Glory – A Preview of Things to Come
By Warren Henderson
Copyright © 2014

Cover Design: John Nicholson
Editor: James Martin
Illustrations: Nathanael Martin
Technical Review: David Dunlap, Steve Hulshizer
Proofreaders: David Lindstrom, Dan Macy

Published by Warren A. Henderson
3769 Indiana Road
Pomona, KS 66076

Perfect Bound ISBN 978-1-939770-24-0
eBook ISBN 978-1-939770-25-7

ORDERING INFORMATION:
Gospel Folio Press
Phone 1-905-835-9166
E-mail: order@gospelfolio.com
Also available in many online retail stores

Printed in the United States

Other Books by the Author

Contents

Preface

The whole Bible is an expression of divine truth. Our understanding of that truth is not gained by the private interpretation of any one particular Scripture (2 Pet. 1:20), but rather through the guidance of the Holy Spirit in comparing Scripture with Scripture (1 Cor. 2:13). In the realm of eschatology (i.e., the study of last things) this task is daunting, and there is little doubt that in heaven we all, including the author, will learn that we did not have everything quite right. With that said, by reviewing the whole of Scripture, we are able to answer with a high degree of confidence such questions as: Does God have a future plan to bless the Jewish nation of Israel? How does His agenda for the Jewish people differ from His future plans for the Church? Is the Church to be looking for the coming of the Antichrist or Christ Himself? Has Christ already come for the Church? Is it true that Christ will not return until the Church prepares His kingdom?

A literal interpretation of Scripture naturally leads to a literal fulfillment of Bible prophecy. Accordingly, many yet unfulfilled Bible prophecies simply call our attention to a future day in which God will honor His Word. Consequently, there is no need to spiritualize or allegorize Scripture to help God out – He is fully capable of doing exactly that which He says, when He says, without man diluting the meaning of what He says.

It is not the intent of this study to condemn various eschatological or theological positions, or belittle those associated with them, but rather to examine the prophetic hopes of the people of God. To do so, we will start with considering the overwhelming Scriptural evidence that God has not abandoned the Jewish people. Furthermore, we will see that if Scripture is interpreted literally, God's future plan for glorifying the Church is quite different than His agenda for restoring the nation of Israel to a position of honor and blessing. Hosea refers to this latter event as *"a door of hope"* for Israel (Hos. 2:15). But we will see that

1

such evidence not only bestows hope to the Jewish nation, but should also excite every Christian to love *"the blessed hope,"* the appearing of the Lord Jesus Christ (2 Tim. 4:8)! Consequently, both the nation of Israel and the Church have all their hopes in Christ!

Writing to encourage persecuted believers scattered throughout the Roman Empire, Peter conveys a message of hope:

> *Blessed be the God and Father of our Lord Jesus Christ, who according to His abundant mercy has begotten us again to **a living hope through the resurrection of Jesus Christ from the dead**, to an inheritance incorruptible and undefiled and that does not fade away, reserved in heaven for you, who are kept by the power of God through faith for salvation ready to be revealed in the last time* (1 Pet. 1:3-5).

> *Therefore gird up the loins of your mind, be sober, and **rest your hope fully upon the grace that is to be brought to you at the revelation of Jesus Christ**; as obedient children, not conforming yourselves to the former lusts, as in your ignorance* (1 Pet. 1:13f).

The King James Version of the Bible renders the phrase referring to hope in verse 13 as *"hope to the end"* and the verses base that hope on the resurrection and revelation of Christ.

Paul also declares that the believer's hope is based on Christ: *"To them God willed to make known what are the riches of the glory of this mystery among the Gentiles: which is Christ in you, the hope of glory"* (Col. 1:27). In Christ, the believer is ensured an extraordinary future!

Solomon declares, *"Hope deferred makes the heart sick"* (Prov. 13:12). Hope is rejoicing now in the future promises of God. What guarded David's heart from depression in difficult times? Hope! And David's hope was solely in the Lord (Ps. 39:7). Jeremiah, who intimately knew about suffering for the Lord, rightly summarizes the matter of hope for all of God's people: *"Blessed is the man who trusts in the Lord, and whose hope is the Lord"* (Jer. 17:7). Trusting and hoping are two different things. However, exercising faith in the present is inseparably tied to hoping for the future. No matter what darkness the future holds, may the Lord's people maintain *"the hope of glory"* and *"hope to the end."*

2

Israel's Hope –
Christ's Second Advent

Israel - The Apple of God's Eye

The ancient idiom *the apple of my eye* is an expression of endearment still commonly used today. What most do not realize is that the term originates in the Old Testament. The Oxford English Dictionary states that the phrase refers to "something or someone that one cherishes above all others."[1] The pupil, or aperture, through which light passes to the retina, is the tenderest part of the eye. Because sight is the most valued of our five senses, we treasure our eyes and diligently guard them from harm. The eye is an incredible organ to which even the slightest injury is most acutely felt and may cause loss of function. It is also an organ that is not easily repaired through surgery once damaged. For these and other reasons our eyes are quite dear to us!

Accordingly, we understand that when Jehovah invokes the term *the apple of God's eye* in Scripture, He is speaking of something or someone that He cherishes greatly. The Lord uses the term three times in the Old Testament and, in each case, He is conveying His tender affection towards the nation of Israel:

> *He found him in a desert land and in the wasteland, a howling wilderness; He encircled him, He instructed him, He kept him as the apple of His eye* (Deut. 32:10).

After Jeremiah announces that God has put Israel away as an adulterous wife he pleads: *"Their heart cried unto the Lord, O wall of the daughter of Zion, let tears run down like a river day and night: give thyself no rest; let not the apple of thine eye cease"* (Lam. 2:18; KJV).

> *For thus says the Lord of hosts: "He sent Me after glory, to the nations which plunder you; for he who touches you touches the apple of His eye"* (Zech. 2:8).

This Old Testament Hebrew idiom is derived from three different Hebrew words. In Deuteronomy 32:10, *'iyshown* literally means "the little man of the eye" (or more specifically the *'iysh* or "man" reflected in the pupil of the eye). The root word in Lamentations 2:18, *'ayin*, literally and figuratively refers to "an eye." Finally, in Zechariah 2:8, *babah* is used to speak of the "gate of the eye" (referring again to the pupil). These words relate to the minute reflection that an onlooker sees when gazing directly into another's eye while face to face. This Hebrew idiom is surprisingly close to the Latin version, *pupilla*, which means a little doll. The pupil is round, dark, and in the center of the eye, and thus reflects an image of what is directly in front of it.

The tenderness of this term is explained in the Song of Solomon. The bridegroom proclaims of his Shulamite bride, *"Behold, you are fair, my love! Behold, you are fair! You have dove's eyes"* (SOS 4:1). The bride speaks of her beloved as having *"eyes like the eyes of doves"* (SOS 5:12). As C.E. Hocking comments in his book *Rise Up My Love*:

> The dove spoken of here is the "rock pigeon," which hides away from danger among the stony crevices of a rock face. Normally, like eyes, these doves are always seen in pairs. Both lovers describe the other's eyes as doves' eyes. Indeed, her eyes are a true mirror image of his and his eyes of hers. Beauty and constancy are suggested, for the dove has its mate alone before its eyes, and mourns when its mate is absent.[2]

Solomon affirms that a husband and wife are to have doves' eyes for each other (i.e., eyes only for each other). If one's love is intensely focused on their spouse, they cannot be distracted by another; to do so would require one to turn their head away from his or her beloved. Hence, in the verses above, the term *apple of one's eye* is an intimate phrase expressing God's concentrated devotion and commitment for His covenant people, the Jews. It is used three times to express God's love for them: at their national commencement (Deut. 32:10), during the darkness of spiritual apostasy in Jeremiah's day (Lam. 2:18), and, lastly, in reference to their spiritual restoration in the Kingdom Age (Zech. 2:8).

Some may take issue with the latter statement, but let us examine the context of Zechariah 2 to confirm the future nature of the passage:

For thus says the Lord of hosts: "He sent Me after glory, to the nations which plunder you; for he who touches you touches the apple of His eye. For surely I will shake My hand against them, and they shall become spoil for their servants. Then you will know that the Lord of hosts has sent Me. "Sing and rejoice, O daughter of Zion! For behold, I am coming and I will dwell in your midst," says the Lord. "Many nations shall be joined to the Lord in that day, and they shall become My people. And I will dwell in your midst. Then you will know that the Lord of hosts has sent Me to you. And the Lord will take possession of Judah as His inheritance in the Holy Land, and will again choose Jerusalem. Be silent, all flesh, before the Lord, for He is aroused from His holy habitation!" (Zech. 2:8-13).

When does God refer to Israel as "the apple of His eye" in this passage? At a future time when the Jewish Messiah will return to the earth to restore His covenant people to Himself and punish those nations who have persecuted them. He will then dwell in the midst of the Jewish people at Jerusalem in the Holy Land, at which time many Gentiles will also be joined to Christ and honor Him. Clearly, this event has not happened yet, but speaks of a literal kingdom that Christ will establish on earth in a future day.

Revelation 20 states six times that this kingdom will last one thousand years and will commence directly after the Antichrist is destroyed (Rev. 19:17-20), those who sided with him are punished (Matt. 13:47-49; 24:31-41; Rev. 19:21), the seven-year Tribulation period is complete (Dan. 9:25-27; 12:7-12; Rev. 12:5-6, 14; 13:5), and Satan and his angels are bound in a bottomless pit (Rev. 20:1-3).

The prophet Zechariah, writing in the sixth century BC, repeatedly mentions the coming of Messiah to rescue and restore His covenant people and includes many prophetic details to ensure that these future events cannot be confused with any past situation. The following are some specific examples of events prophesied by Zechariah which have not occurred yet:

Zechariah 8:20-22: Jerusalem will be the religious capital of the world – all those entering the millennial kingdom will journey to Jerusalem to worship and pray to the Lord.

Zechariah 8:23: During the millennial kingdom, the Jews will be the most esteemed nation on earth (also Isa. 61:9).

Zechariah 12:2-9: Just prior to the Kingdom Age, all the nations of the earth will gather against the Jews and Jerusalem will be under siege. The Lord will defend His people by striking the enemy horses with blindness and their riders with madness. The Lord will destroy all the nations gathered against Jerusalem (also see Joel 3).

Zechariah 12:10: When Messiah returns to defend His covenant people, the Jews will look upon Him and weep; they will then realize that they had previously crucified their Messiah, as prophesied in Psalm 22, Isaiah 53, and Zechariah 13:7.

Zechariah 13:8-9: Two-thirds of the Jewish people will die during the Tribulation Period because of the Antichrist's intense persecution of them. The remaining third will be protected from harm (Isa. 1:18; Rev. 12:5-6, 13-17), experience spiritual rebirth (Joel 2:28-29; Ezek. 36:23-28), and be restored to their Messiah, the Lord Jesus Christ (Rom. 9:27). In fact, 144,000 Jews, 12,000 from each of twelve tribes, will be specifically sealed and protected by God to preach the kingdom gospel message throughout the entire world during the Tribulation (Matt. 24:14; Rev. 7:4-8; 14:1-5).

Zechariah 14: The city of Jerusalem will have been conquered (half its people enslaved) when Christ returns from heaven to protect His people and destroy the Antichrist (vv. 2-3). He will land on the Mount of Olives and split the mountain in half, such that a river of water will flow to the east and to the west out of the newly formed ravine (vv. 4-8). The returning Messiah will be King over the whole earth (v. 9). He will cause the Jews' oppressors to fight each other and then cause their bodies to dissolve where they stand (vv. 12-13). John provides the number of those soldiers gathered in the Jezreel Valley for the battle of Armageddon: 200,000,000 (Rev. 9:16). He then explains that the entire valley will become a giant winepress, for when Christ destroys this great army, their blood will freely flow out of its basin for 182 miles (Rev. 14:19-20). Zechariah notes that the Jews will be fighting to defend Jerusalem when Christ returns and then He will bestow on them the wealth of the nations (vv. 14-15). Afterwards, says Zechariah, all the people remaining on the earth will be required to come to Jerusalem to worship the Messiah and they will be severely punished if they do not (vv. 16-21).

It is quite obvious to even a casual reader that these events have never occurred. For example, the Mount of Olives is still intact, Jerusalem is not the religious capital of the world, and the nations do not worship the Jewish Messiah there. The context of the passage is plainly future and Jewish in nature, thus it cannot be referring to the Church.

Throughout his entire book, Zechariah distinctly references the Jews as the people of Judah (21 times), the Jewish nation of Israel (five times), and those living in the literal city of Jerusalem (41 times). He speaks of the Jewish people in the second person ("you") while referring to non-Jews as "they." Zechariah also describes them as those who orchestrated the crucifixion of their Messiah and who, at His Second Advent, will mourn they did so (Zech. 12:10). Only seriously flawed hermeneutics could spiritualize all these references and fail to see the Jewish flavor of this book.

The Jews referred to in the book of Zechariah are the same Jews as in the rest of the Old Testament. They are not the Church. The Israel that Zechariah refers to is the Jewish nation whose capital is Jerusalem. If God has no plan for the nation of Israel, why does He still refer to them as "the apple of His eye" at the very moment He will return to avenge them among the nations, exalt them as His esteemed people, and take up residence among them again?

Though presently rebellious, Israel is the apple of God's eye and Zechariah warned that any nation that oppresses God's covenant people will receive His wrath! Corrie Ten Boom's father, Casper, realized this truth. Adolph Hitler hated the Jews and was intent upon exterminating them; over six million Jews were murdered during the World War II era. But in the early days of World War II, the Ten Boom family hid Jews in their home and assisted them to escape Nazi-occupied Holland. Eventually, the Ten Boom family was arrested and imprisoned for their compassionate ministry to the Jewish people. Most of the family died in labor camps, but Corrie survived. She later wrote of her family's experience and why her father had compassion for the Jewish people:

> Once the occupation of Holland was underway and the Jews began to suffer persecution, Casper, although quite old by then, devoted himself to the rescue effort. He even attempted to get his own yellow Star of David to wear, so he could identify with the Jews in their time of trouble. Although Corrie kept him from doing so, he compensated by

9

taking off his hat to every Jew he would meet.[3] He surprised Corrie by his comment when he saw the soldiers packing Jews into the back of a truck: "Those poor people," he lamented. Corrie thought he meant the Jews, but then he continued, "I pity the poor Germans, Corrie. They have touched the apple of God's eye."[4]

Consequently, the Nazi movement was defeated, and the German people suffered much during Hitler's leadership and afterwards. Jehovah still loves and will always love His covenant people. The Jewish people are the apple of God's eye. Any nation who persecutes them will inevitably reap God's fury (Jer. 2:3; Zech. 2:8)!

Thankfully, many of the nations with a Christian heritage have been friendly towards Israel and have reaped the blessings promised to those who are (Gen. 12:3). The United States has been a major advocate of Israel even before its national reestablishment. It was President Harry S. Truman who stood up for Israel after World War II and requested Britain to remove its naval blockade around Israel and let the Jews return home. Just a day prior to the expiration of the British Mandate, Truman recognized the state of Israel on May 14, 1948, eleven minutes after the Jews declared themselves to be a nation.[5] The armies of four Arab nations, Egypt, Syria, Transjordan, and Iraq, entered into what had been British Mandate Palestine and launched the 1948 Arab-Israeli War. Truman later explained why he supported the creation of a Jewish nation in Palestine:

> Hitler had been murdering Jews right and left. I saw it, and I dream about it even to this day. The Jews needed some place where they could go. It is my attitude that the American government couldn't stand idly by while the victims [of] Hitler's madness are not allowed to build new lives.[6]

After a year of intense fighting, a ceasefire was brokered and temporary borders for the nation were defined. Shortly after this, the United Nations voted to admit Israel as the fifty-ninth member of the United Nations by a majority vote on May 11, 1949. Israel is the apple of God's eye, and any nation that treats them poorly will be judged by God. Hopefully, we Christians will never lose sight of this important fact!

Allegories of Love

God understands our natural limitations in comprehending supernatural and timeless realities. Therefore He graciously employs various literary forms in Scripture to teach us of Himself. Consequently, Jehovah's tender love for His covenant people is not only revealed in the plain language of Scripture, or applied Hebrew idioms, such as *the apple of My eye*, but also through allegory (e.g. Gal. 4:24). An allegory is a story which illustrates a hidden or symbolic meaning. John Bunyan's *Pilgrim's Progress* of 1678 is a well-known literary example of a Christian allegory.

Jehovah reveals several scriptural allegories to express His special and unique relationship with the Jewish people. Moses directly informed the Jews that they were a "special people" to God, above all other people groups on the earth (Deut. 7:6). This special union is expressed through several sincere allegorical expressions. For example, the Jews are *"the sheep of His pasture"* (Ps. 100:3) and His *"peculiar treasure"* (Ex. 19:5). Some of these emblematic declarations pertain to relationships. For instance, God refers to Israel as a firstborn son, a betrothed virgin, and a restored and forgiven unfaithful wife. Through each of these metaphors, Jehovah conveys His steadfast devotion to the Jewish people in terms that we can readily relate to.

The Sheep of His Pasture

God wants all of humanity to know Him and to appreciate Him for who He is, not who we think He is. It is for this reason that the psalmist reminds the Jewish nation of the reason they were created: *"Know that the Lord, He is God; it is He who has made us, and not we ourselves; we are His people and the sheep of His pasture"* (Ps. 100:3). It was not enough for the Jews to merely know that God existed, or even that they were God's sheep; God wanted them to understand that He loved them

11

and longed to care for them and He wanted them to both know and rest in His love.

The Peculiar Treasure

Through the seven Kingdom Parables recorded in Matthew 13, the Lord Jesus outlines the future of Israel: In the fifth of the Kingdom Parables, Christ alludes to this: *"Again, the kingdom of heaven is like treasure hidden in a field, which a man found and hid; and for joy over it he goes and sells all that he has and buys that field"* (Matt. 13:44). God considers Israel a treasure for Himself (Ex. 19:5; Ps. 135:4). It seems, then, that what is pictured in this parable is the spiritual blindness of the Jewish nation. They were cut off from God for rejecting Christ who then turned to woo a Gentile bride for Himself. This treasure (the Jewish nation) was therefore hidden again in a field (i.e., among the nations of the world). Later, at the Lord's second coming, He will identify with His people again and will be accepted by them (Zech. 12:10). At that time, they will receive the Holy Spirit and a new heart and be restored to Jehovah.

Sarah, as the mother of the promised son, provides an illustration of the nation of Israel. For this reason, it is significant then that she is the only woman in all of Scripture whose age at the time of her death is recorded, 127 years. Sarah's age at death allows us to determine Isaac's corresponding age when his mother died; he was 37 years old. Isaac grieved the loss of his mother three years before taking an unseen bride, Rebekah, from the foreign land of Mesopotamia, at which point he was comforted (Gen. 24:57-67). It is noted that the Lord Jesus preached to the nation of Israel for three years and sorrowfully wept over their rejection of Him. After His resurrection, the Lord was blessed by the spiritual union of the Church, which is mainly a Gentile bride (Acts 2; Eph. 5:23-33). Obviously, Sarah cannot be resurrected to picture the spiritual rebirth of the Jewish nation; rather, this truth is pictured when Abraham takes another wife, Keturah, who bears him six sons. Abraham then bestows all that he has on his son, Isaac, picturing the Millennial Kingdom of Christ (Gen. 25:1-5).

The events surrounding Sarah's death and Isaac's marriage and inheritance convey a prophetic portrait of God's future dealing with the nation of Israel. He plans to regather the Jews to the land of Israel and then dwell among them again. In fact, the prophet Ezekiel states that Jehovah will not leave one Jew dispersed among the nations (Ezek. 39:28-29). In that day, God's peculiar treasure will be fully recovered from where He had hidden it centuries earlier.

The Firstborn Son

Jehovah first explained the importance of this relationship to Moses at the burning bush (Ex. 4:21-22). God had adopted the nation of Israel (Rom. 9:4); He considered them to be a firstborn son to Him—they had a place of privilege among the nations.

Through Jehovah's covenant with Abraham, Israel had been singled out from among the nations as a special object of God's favor: *"For I am a Father to Israel, and Ephraim is My firstborn"* (Jer. 31:9). The firstborn son had a privileged position in the family, including the right of family leadership and the greatest share of inheritance. The nation's continued rejection of Messiah has delayed, but not cancelled, its entry into its inheritance, *"for the gifts and calling of God are irrevocable"* (Rom. 11:29). In fact, this very passage tells us that the hardening of Israel is temporary (*"until the fullness of the Gentiles has come in,"* v. 25), not permanent. Jehovah will not fail to give His firstborn his inheritance.

The Betrothed Virgin

In Ezekiel 16, the nation of Israel is likened to a discarded newborn girl whom God rescues from certain death. After gently picking her up from a field, the Lord washes her, nurtures her, and protects her from harm (Ezek. 16:3-7). After she reaches the age of maturity, He then confirms a marriage covenant with her that speaks of the new relationship that He wanted with Israel:

> *"When I passed by you again and looked upon you, indeed your time was the time of love; so I spread My wing over you and covered your nakedness. Yes, I swore an oath to you and entered into a covenant with you, and you became Mine," says the Lord God* (Ezek. 16:8).

Jehovah's passion for Israel – his wife through covenant – is poetically described in this verse. The Hebrew word for "love" in this verse is *dowd*, meaning "to boil" (i.e., figuratively: "to love" and, by implication, "a lover"). This word is rendered "love" seven times in the Old Testament and always confers the sense of a boiling pot of fervent passion between a husband and his wife (not necessarily sexually). Jehovah uses wondrously intimate language to express His affection and devotion to the Jewish nation.

Unfortunately, Israel later forsook the Lord and embraced false gods. Israel's spiritual adultery provoked Jehovah to jealousy; He responded by writing her a bill of divorcement and put her away to be punished among the nations (Ezek. 16:38; Jer. 3:8). But that is not the end of the story!

The Restored Wife

Despite the unfaithfulness of Israel to Jehovah, the Lord is moved with compassion and mercy to restore her to a place of special intimacy, likened to that of marital companionship. Jehovah moved several prophets to pronounce His promise to restore the Jewish nation as His faithful wife in a future day:

"Nevertheless I will remember My covenant with you in the days of your youth, and I will establish an everlasting covenant with you. Then you will remember your ways and be ashamed ... I will establish My covenant with you. Then you shall know that I am the Lord, that you may remember and be ashamed, and never open your mouth anymore because of your shame, when I provide you an atonement for all you have done," says the Lord God (Ezek. 16:60-63).

"I will punish her for the days of the Baals to which she burned incense. She decked herself with her earrings and jewelry, and went after her lovers; but Me she forgot," says the Lord. "'Therefore, behold, I will allure her, will bring her into the wilderness, and speak comfort to her" (Hos. 2:14-15). *"I will betroth you to Me forever; yes, I will betroth you to Me in righteousness and justice, in lovingkindness and mercy; I will betroth you to Me in faithfulness, and you shall know the Lord"* (Hos. 2:19-20).

"For I am with you," says the Lord, "to save you; though I make a full end of all nations where I have scattered you, yet I will not make a complete end of you. But I will correct you in justice, and will not

let you go altogether unpunished" (Jer. 30:11). *"You shall be my people, and I will be your God"* (Jer. 30:22).

The prophet Hosea was allowed to experience the unfaithfulness of his wife, Gomer, to illustrate not only the Lord's heartbreak, but also His resolve to be reconciled with His wayward people. Even after Gomer had embraced her lovers for the provisions Hosea had secretly provided for her, God commanded him to redeem her and take her back as his wife. He did so. After her lovers had abused and abandoned Gomer, she was sold in a common slave market (likely humiliated by being stripped bare); there Hosea bought his own adulterous wife for fifteen pieces of silver and a homer and half of barley (Hos. 3:2). Hosea then said to her: *"You shall stay with me many days; you shall not play the harlot, nor shall you have a man – so, too, will I be toward you"* (Hos. 3:3). Then the prophet immediately connected his own marital situation with the future relationship of Jehovah and His covenant people:

> *For the children of Israel shall abide many days without king or prince, without sacrifice or sacred pillar, without ephod or teraphim. Afterward the children of Israel shall return and seek the Lord their God and David their king. They shall fear the Lord and His goodness in the latter days* (Hos. 3:4-5).

Gomer did not forsake Hosea again and neither will God's covenant people when they are restored in the latter days. The Mosaic Law did not contain a provision of forgiveness for adultery – offenders, like Gomer, were to be put to death. But Hosea's dealings with his unfaithful wife demonstrate that God would have a provision for grace which the Law could not extend. Through a new and everlasting covenant, He could forgive Israel's sin. Jehovah could righteously restore Israel to Himself because He punished His own Son in her place. This covenant was secured at Calvary and was sealed by the blood of the Lord Jesus Christ *"with the house of Israel and house of Judah"* (Heb. 8:8) as prophesied in Jeremiah 31:31-32. What would be the spiritual benefit of this New Covenant? Speaking for Jehovah, Jeremiah answers:

*"But this is the covenant that I will make with the house of Israel af-
ter those days, says the Lord: I will put My law in their minds, and
write it on their hearts; and I will be their God, and they shall be My
people. No more shall every man teach his neighbor, and every man
his brother, saying, 'Know the Lord,' for they all shall know Me,
from the least of them to the greatest of them, says the Lord. For I
will forgive their iniquity, and their sin I will remember no more"*
(Jer. 31:33-34).

Thankfully, as Paul explains in Ephesians 2:11-3:7, Gentile believers are a second benefactor of this covenant and are permitted to share
in all the blessings promised to the Jewish nation. They are the wild
branches grafted into the tree representing the blessings of Christ root-
ed in God's covenant with Abraham in Genesis 12:1-3 (cf. Rom. 11:17-
20). The New Covenant permits individual Jews to be saved now and
the Jewish nation as a whole to be reconciled with Jehovah at a future
date.

As reported by Jeremiah, the very laws of nature are a guarantee
that the Lord will preserve Israel (Jer. 31:35). He then states that *"If
those ordinances depart from before Me, says the Lord, then the seed of
Israel shall also cease from being a nation before Me forever"* (Jer.
31:36). Every glimpse of sky and sea should remind us that, by Jehovah's own decree, the Jewish nation will be before Him forever. Presently, they have been given over to spiritual blindness because of their
rejection of Christ (Rom. 11:9-11) and God is using Gentile believers
to provoke them to jealousy (Rom. 11:11-15). But Paul explains that
when the Church is complete, God will restore His covenant people to
Himself:

*That blindness in part has happened to Israel until the fullness of the
Gentiles has come in. And so all Israel will be saved, as it is written:
"The Deliverer will come out of Zion, and He will turn away ungod-
liness from Jacob; for this is My covenant with them, when I take
away their sins"* (Rom. 11:25-27).

The immense love of God for His covenant people, even in their
backslidden condition, is shown five times in Jeremiah 3 in His call for
the Jewish nation to repent and to be restored to Him (Jer. 3:12-14, 20-

24). While the message is primarily directed at Judah (the two southern tribes), God still longed to be reunited with Israel (the northern ten tribes), even after one hundred years of dispersion and captivity. Approximately a century before Jeremiah called Judah to repentance, Jehovah confirmed His love for the northern tribes, in spite of their blatant idolatry and subsequent captivity in Assyria:

> *You whom I have taken from the ends of the earth, and called from its farthest regions, and said to you, "You are My servant, I have chosen you and have not cast you away: Fear not, for I am with you; be not dismayed, for I am your God. I will strengthen you, yes, I will help you, I will uphold you with My righteous right hand"* (Isa. 41:9-10).

Although their hearts were not with Jehovah, His heart was still with them. He promised to accompany them and sustain them through their disciplinary judgment. He loved His covenant people too much to leave them in their pagan exile, and thus sought to purify them and restore them to Himself. Jeremiah also employs the allegories of the marital relationship (Jer. 3:12) and the parent-child relationship (Jer. 3:14) in his messages to Judah. This conveys to the Jews a twofold certainty of their relational acceptance with Jehovah, even though their sinful practices have resulted in an extended break of fellowship.

Grace and Faith from the Beginning

Many Christians today believe that there are no scriptural promises remaining for the Jewish people. Consequently, Israel has no claim to the Promised Land and God's unfulfilled promises to her have been somehow transferred to the Church. This doctrine is called "Replacement Theology." Dr. Barnhouse summarized its teaching: "The amillennarians take all the promises that belong to the Jews and apply them to the Church, leaving the curses, as Satan likes to do, for the Jews."[1] Replacement Theology denies the Jews any opportunity for divine restoration as God's covenant people, a peaceful residence in the Promised Land, or a status of honor in Christ's future kingdom. This teaching coincides with that of several prominent cults.

In this respect, Replacement Theology has struck a common chord with the Muslim world – both believe that the Jewish state has no biblical reason for existing today. Most of those who hold to covenantal or reformed theology frameworks (these will be explained later) believe that the Church is the Israel of today and that God has abandoned the Jewish nation forever. Proponents of this view would argue that God has carefully chosen His people throughout the ages and that because of their repetitious rebellion, the Jewish people are no longer His chosen people.

Covenant theology also teaches that there is no literal, future, millennial kingdom of Christ, but that Christ's kingdom exists spiritually within the Church today. While it is true that the kingdom of God exists in a spiritual sense within the Church today, this cannot be equated to the literal, earthly kingdom which is prophetically foretold in numerous Scriptures. Such a conclusion is only possible by a dual hermeneutic which figuratively interprets large portions of the Bible, especially those passages which are eschatological in nature. In other words, prophecies related to Israel are treated as allegories in order to render them applicable to the Church now.

19

One fourth of the Bible is prophetic in content and the great majority of these prophecies pertain to the Jewish people. Prophets were usually summoned by God to confront the Jewish apostasy of their day. However, in doing so, God usually pronounced promises of future blessing and restoration in order to instill hope into the hearts of the faithful during periods of intense disciplinary suffering. Consequently, although God unquestionably has but one means to save sinners throughout history (i.e., through Christ), the entire Bible shows that God's dealings with the nation of Israel are quite different than His dealings with the Church. Let us navigate from Genesis to Revelation to better understand the unfolding of this essential truth.

In the Beginning

The book of Genesis records the beginning of the world as it pertains to man, the beginning of man through Adam, the new beginning for man after the flood through Noah, and the beginning of a chosen nation (Israel) in Abram, who was later renamed Abraham.

We need not read more than six chapters in our Bibles to learn that the general populace had become utterly depraved: *"Wickedness of man was great in the earth, and that every intent of the thoughts of his heart was only evil continually"* (Gen. 6:5). God's solution to wholesale human rebellion follows: *"I will destroy man whom I have created from the face of the earth ... but Noah found grace in the eyes of the Lord"* (Gen. 6:7-8). Noah was not a sinless man, but he *"was a just man, perfect in his generations"* and he *"walked with God"* (Gen. 6:9-10). God chose to extend Noah grace and to reveal His plan for humanity to him. Noah then proved his faith by building the huge Ark that God had commanded, even though there was no reasonable means of validating the forthcoming deluge (Heb. 11:7). As a result, he and his family were saved from the wrath of God which wiped out the rest of humanity.

For over 400 years after the flood, God endured a pagan world in silence. Then, suddenly, the God of glory appeared to a man named Abram, living in Ur (i.e., Mesopotamia). Until Genesis 12, God had been dealing with mankind as a whole; but in Genesis 12, He chose to focus His sovereign dealings on the life of one man. Through Abram would come both the written Word of God and the Living Word of life, the Messiah.

Despite mankind's overall propensity to rebel, God chose to bestow mercy again on humanity by making another covenant. On this occasion, it was not made with humanity in general, but with one man, Abram, and his seed. In Genesis 9, God had made a conditional pledge to all humanity. However, human conscience (Gen. 3) and human government (Gen. 9) were insufficient agents to ensure human morality; thus, mankind forfeited the blessings of God. So God then chose to extend an unconditional promise through one man to bless all the families of the earth (Gen. 12:3). The blessing would ultimately come through Christ and would be imparted to all those who would embrace God's revealed truth, at any particular time, by faith.

Joshua informs us that Abram was an idol worshipper (Josh. 24:2). Accordingly, Moses identifies him as *"a Syrian ready to perish"* (Deut. 26:5). Though an idol worshipper ready to perish, Stephen informs us in Acts 7 that *"the God of Glory"* appeared to Abram in Ur and called Abram away from Ur to a land He would give him. God made a sovereign choice to bring forth the Messiah through Abram. So, God called a pagan named Abram to leave his country, to separate from his kindred, and to go forth to inherit a land he had never seen – and Abram did just that!

God made an unconditional covenant to bring blessing to the world and for Abram to be an instrument of salvation. Because Abram believed God, God could use him as a fit and faithful example of a pilgrim, elevate his name among men, forge a nation from him, and award him a land of his own. The choice of Abram to believe God's revealed truth and to reject the social pull of Ur accomplished for him what it does for an individual today when they believe the gospel and reject the wisdom and toxic influence of the world. Namely, it makes him a worshipper of God and a citizen of heaven and, thus, a pilgrim and a stranger on earth as God's witness.

The wonder of Abram's power is revealed in one word which first appears in the Bible in Genesis 14:13; the word is *Hebrew*. It means "the passenger," and it beautifully encapsulates the pilgrimage of Abram and the fact that he was a stranger in a world that was estranged to God. Because of his demonstrated faith, God promised childless

21

Abraham that He would rear up a special nation through a unique son to be born of his elderly wife, Sarah. This son's name was to be Isaac (Gen. 17:19; 18:10-14). Isaac would have a son named Jacob whom God renamed Israel (Gen. 32:28; 35:9-12). The Jewish nation experienced its expansion through Jacob, thus the children of Israel became the tribes of Israel (Gen. 49:28) and, eventually, the nation of Israel (Ex. 3:16; 4:22).

God performed no signs and wonders for Abram. He simply reconfirmed His word to him. But that was good enough for Abram – he simply trusted God and believed. God responded by accrediting a standing of righteousness to Abram's account. This accrediting, or accounting, of divine righteousness to a sinner who exercises faith is seen throughout the Bible and is thoroughly explained by the apostle Paul in Romans 4 and 5. Obviously, God wanted no confusion on this matter for the words "believe," "counted," and "righteousness" all occur for the first time in the Bible in one verse (Gen. 15:6) and in one Divine declaration just after the first reference of "the word of the Lord" in the Bible (Gen. 15:1). Genesis 15:6 appears three times in the New Testament: Romans 4:3, Galatians 3:6, and James 2:23. In Abraham's case, what preceded imputed righteousness? His faith. In Noah's case, what preceded imputed righteousness? God's grace. Combining these two important truths we have *"For by grace are ye saved through faith; and that not of yourselves, it is the gift of God"* (Eph. 2:8). Both God's means of salvation through grace and man's responsibility to lay hold of this gift by personal faith are clearly presented in Genesis and throughout the Bible.

A Wider Promise

While God's covenant with Abraham bestowed a special land on his descendants, Abram was also given a much wider promise: *"in you shall all families of the earth be blessed."* God's covenant with Abram has its ultimate fulfillment in the redemptive work of Christ, a descendant of Abram. But even before that ultimate fulfillment, Uriah the Hittite, Caleb the Kenizzite, Ruth the Moabite, and Tamar and Rahab of the Canaanites are some of the Gentiles who received divine blessing by trusting Abraham's God. Through faith, God is willing to declare the wonders of His grace to anyone, anywhere, and at any time. Paul

22

puts the matter this way: *"For the grace of God that brings salvation hath appeared to all men"* (Titus 2:11) and God *"is long suffering towards us, not willing that any should perish, but that all should come to repentance"* (2 Pet. 3:9). Faith is the ability of the soul to reach beyond what can be verified by the human senses and trust what we cannot confirm by our own understanding (Heb. 11:3). This is why one must have faith to please God, *"for without faith it is impossible to please Him"* (Heb. 11:6).

When Joshua led the Israelites into Canaan, the inhabitants of Canaan had a choice: they could either oppose Jehovah or they could humble themselves and worship Him. The fact that immoral Rahab, from the lowest social class in Canaanite society, could be saved meant that anyone could have received mercy (Josh. 2). The grace shown to Rahab was in fact available to all the inhabitants of the land, for God had told Abraham centuries earlier, *"in you shall all families of the earth be blessed"* (Gen. 12:3). Jehovah had granted Abraham the title deed of all the land between the Euphrates River and the Mediterranean Sea. Although Abraham did not come into possession of his full inheritance in his lifetime, his descendants eventually would, and, would therefore also rule over the ten people groups listed in Genesis 15:19-21 (which included the Canaanites, Rahab's people). This meant that as this prophecy unfolded in time, these people groups would be exposed to the truth of God's plan and would have an opportunity to be blessed through Abraham. To enter into this blessing, it would be necessary to submit by faith to God's rule and to surrender to His people, as Rahab did.

What Paul declares in the New Testament was therefore certainly true in the Old Testament as well: *"For the grace of God that brings salvation hath appeared to all men"* (Titus 2:11). The nations mentioned in Genesis 15 were not hopelessly condemned; there was a way of escape for them through faith. By identifying with and honoring Abraham's descendants, the pagan inhabitants of the land could both know and be reconciled to Abraham's God.

By faith, Rahab escaped certain destruction and was incorporated into the commonwealth of Israel. Thus, Gentiles, such as Rahab, benefitted from the privileges and responsibilities of God's covenant people during Old Testament times. Gentiles during the Church Age similarly receive the covenant blessings promised Abraham through Christ: *"Remember that you once Gentiles in the flesh ... that at that time you were without Christ, being aliens from the commonwealth of Israel and strangers from the covenants of promise, having no hope and without God in the world. But now in Christ Jesus you who once were far off have been brought near by the blood of Christ"* (Eph. 2:11-13). The writer of Hebrews reminds us that *"without faith it is impossible to please Him, for he who comes to God must believe that He is, and that He is a rewarder of those who diligently seek Him"* (Heb. 11:6). Rahab was not exposed to all the divine revelation that you and I have today, but she did respond in faith to that which was revealed to her and God rewarded her richly.

Today, through the gospel of the Lord Jesus Christ, both Jews and Gentiles are being added to a spiritual temple called the Church (Eph. 2:11-22). There is no distinction between Jew and Gentile within this Body, for, in Christ, all become heirs of the promises God made to Abraham.

But the nation of Israel is composed of the physical descendants of Abraham through Isaac and Jacob. The covenant promising specific blessings, such as land, to Abraham and his physical descendants was also affirmed with Isaac (Gen. 26:2-5) and Jacob (Gen. 28:13-15; 35:10-12).

God said, Sarah thy wife shall bear thee a son indeed; and thou shalt call his name Isaac: and I will establish My covenant with him for an everlasting covenant, and with his seed after him (Gen. 17:19).

And behold, the Lord stood above it and said: "I am the Lord God of Abraham your father and the God of Isaac; the land on which you lie I will give to you and your descendants. Also your descendants shall be as the dust of the earth; you shall spread abroad to the west and the east, to the north and the south; and in you and in your seed all the families of the earth shall be blessed. Behold, I am with you and will keep you wherever you go, and will bring you back to this land; for I will not leave you until I have done what I have spoken to you" (Gen. 28:13-15).

And God said to him, "Your name is Jacob; your name shall not be called Jacob anymore, but Israel shall be your name." So He called his name Israel. Also God said to him: "I am God Almighty. Be fruitful and multiply; a nation and a company of nations shall proceed from you, and kings shall come from your body. The land which I gave Abraham and Isaac I give to you; and to your descendants after you I give this land" (Gen. 35:10-12).

This covenant pertains to Abraham's physical lineage through them and is repeatedly said to be everlasting. While the Church enjoys much blessing in Christ because of the Abrahamic covenant, the Church has no specific promise of land – Abraham's descendants through Isaac and Jacob do. Thus, it is important to understand that the Bible speaks of two peoples descending from Abraham: a physical people (the Jews) with the promise of physical blessings, and a spiritual people with spiritual blessings. Paul acknowledged that he was physically born a Jew, *the seed of Abraham* (Rom. 11:1), but had now become a spiritual child of Abraham by exercising faith in the gospel message of Jesus Christ. Paul had experienced spiritual rebirth. He was now justified in Christ and was enjoying the resurrection power and fellowship of Christ's life. The nation of Israel will not obtain this blessing until after the Church Age is complete and the Tribulation Period draws to a close (Rom. 11:25-27).

In the Church Age, all who follow Abraham's example of exercising faith in divinely revealed truth are called *"Abraham's seed"* (Gal. 3:26-29) for Abraham is *"the father of all them that believe, though they be not circumcised"* (Rom. 4:11). Accordingly, the Church is not the Jewish nation, but a spiritual body of Jews and Gentiles who have trusted the gospel message of Jesus Christ. As God promised Abraham, all families of the earth would be blessed in him. This has been fulfilled because Christ, the Messiah, is a progeny of Abraham (Matt. 1:1-17). The nation of Israel, the physical seed of Abraham, and the spiritual seed of Abraham, those justified in Christ by faith, have different promises and distinct blessings.

John's prophetic vision of a future scene in heaven confirms that a vast multitude of redeemed people from every nation, tribe, people group, and language will be before God's throne (Rev. 7:9). Through divine grace and human faith (i.e., trusting in God's revealed Word), the full blessing of the Abrahamic covenant will be realized in a coming day – all families of the earth shall be blessed through Christ. Not all will be saved, but there will be someone from every extended family among the redeemed in heaven.

Summary

After the Church Age is complete, the Lord will again refine and restore His covenant people, the Jews (Rom. 11:25). This time period correlates with the Tribulation Period which concludes with the Second Advent of Christ to the earth. This will be a visible coming in which the entire world will see the glory of Christ (Matt. 24:30; Luke 17:24). This timeframe is also recognized as the final week (i.e., seven years) in Daniel's seventy-week prophecy (Dan. 9:25-27) which will be more thoroughly explained in the next chapter. Clearly, Jehovah cannot be finished with the Jewish nation, for He decreed an everlasting covenant with Abraham's descendants through Jacob. Jehovah is a covenant-keeping God and He has established irrevocable promises that He must fulfill. In so doing, the vast wonders of divine grace and mercy will be witnessed and appreciated by all who trust in the Lord.

Seventy – Israel's Number

At the end of his ministry, Moses warned the Israelites that, if necessary, Jehovah would exile them to purge idolatry from the Promised Land (Deut. 30:1-6). Moses also promised that if God did disperse them among the nations, He would eventually gather them back again into the land. This covenant with the Israelites was therefore conditional – they would be blessed if they obeyed God's commandments and punished if they did not (Jer. 24:9).

Thankfully, God's covenant with Abraham was unconditional (Gen. 12:1-3). This covenant promised blessing and protection to a future, refined nation of his descendants. Eventually, there would be a nation from Abraham's lineage which would inherit all of the Promised Land (Gen. 15:18-21) and be highly esteemed and blessed by all nations (Gen. 12:3). Until that time, the same Scripture that promised the chastening of Israel also guaranteed her restoration. This was to encourage the Jews to flee from idolatry and seek God with all their heart. When they did, God would return them to their homeland and commune with them again (Jer. 24:12-14). God promised His people, *"You will seek me and find me when you seek me with all your heart"* (Jer. 29:13). Unfortunately, there have often been times in their history when the Jews knew *about* Jehovah, but they did not know Him intimately. At such times, God chastened them as a proof of His love for them and to awaken them to His abiding presence.

After Moses, God moved His prophets Isaiah, Jeremiah, Ezekiel, and Daniel to foretell in more detail how the Jews would be dispersed among the nations and then regathered to the Promise Land. Isaiah, as well as Amos and Hosea, warned the ten northern tribes that disciplinary judgment and exile were imminent if they did not repent of their idolatry. They refused to repent and God used the Assyrian empire to execute His justice. After their exile, Isaiah wrote a message of hope to the dispersed Jews:

It shall come to pass in that day that the Lord shall set His hand again the second time to recover the remnant of His people who are left, from Assyria and Egypt, from Pathros and Cush, from Elam and Shinar, from Hamath and the islands of the sea. He will set up a banner for the nations, and will assemble the outcasts of Israel, and gather together the dispersed of Judah from the four corners of the earth (Isa. 11:11-12).

Notice that Isaiah prophesied that the southern kingdom of Judah would be dispersed also; this was fulfilled a century after Isaiah predicted it. But Isaiah also stated that God would gather the entire Jewish nation, both Israel and Judah, back into the land. As we will see momentarily, the southern kingdom did return to the Promised Land after seventy years of exile, but the northern ten tribes have not yet been gathered to their homeland; this part of the prophesy is yet future.

The Number Seventy

The number seventy is associated with the nation of Israel in a special way throughout Scripture. Genesis 46 provides the first roster of the nation, which included the names of those in Jacob's family that traveled with him to Egypt. In all, sixty-six sons and grandsons are named. Counting Joseph and his two sons, who were already in Egypt, and Jacob himself, the total number of males composing the nation of Israel at this time was seventy (Gen. 46:5). There were seventy elders of Israel (Num. 11:16). During New Testament times, there were seventy members of the Sanhedrin and seventy witnesses sent out to Israel by Christ (Luke 10:1). This thread of seventy and Israel can also be seen in the books of Jeremiah and Daniel where it is related to the regathering of the Jewish people to their homeland.

Jeremiah's Seventy-Year Prophecy

A century after Isaiah finished warning the northern kingdom of Israel to repent, Jehovah stirred up the prophets Jeremiah, Zephaniah, and Habakkuk to deliver a stern message to idolatrous Judah, the southern kingdom. Jeremiah faithfully forewarned the people for over forty years that divine retribution was imminent if they did not repent of their pagan ways and cold-hearted religiosity (Jer. 3). Jehovah used the Babylonian Empire as His rod of chastening and decimated Jerusalem, a matter that the prophet Habakkuk had difficulty understanding. Between 605 and 586 BC, many Jews were slaughtered and tens of thousands were hauled away to Babylon as slaves. The temple, the city wall, the palace, and much of Jerusalem were destroyed by the Babylonians in 586 BC.

How long would this judgment and exile last? Jeremiah indicated the interval: *"And this whole land shall be a desolation and an astonishment, and these nations shall serve the king of Babylon seventy years"* (Jer. 25:11). Jeremiah confirmed a twofold seventy-year prophecy concerning the nation of Israel: there would be seventy years of Babylonian captivity and seventy years of rest for the land (v. 11; 2 Chron. 36:21). The seventy years of captivity began the very year that Jeremiah spoke the prophecy, coinciding with Nebuchadnezzar's first invasion of Judah and first deportation of Jews to Babylon in 605 BC. The captivity portion of this prophecy was concluded seventy years later when the Babylonian empire fell to the Medes and Persians in late 538 BC and the Jewish captives were freed by King Cyrus. This event was foretold two centuries earlier by Isaiah (Isa. 44:28-45:1). The prophet Daniel, who had been in that first group of captives, understood this event to be the fulfillment of Jeremiah's prophecy (Dan. 9:2).

The second portion of the prophecy of seventy years did not begin until Nebuchadnezzar's third invasion, when he initiated a siege of Jerusalem during King Zedekiah's reign. God commanded the prophet Ezekiel to record the exact date this occurred:

Again, in the ninth year, in the tenth month, on the tenth day of the month, the word of the Lord came to me, saying, "Son of man, write down the name of the day, this very day – the king of Babylon started his siege against Jerusalem this very day" (Ezek. 24:1-2).

This date is the equivalent of December 13, 589 BC. in the Gregorian Calendar. Why did the Lord want the exact date of the beginning of the siege of Jerusalem identified? Because it was the day that all agriculture stopped in Judah. The Chaldean army sowed fields with rocks, filled wells with debris, destroyed vineyards and fruit groves, and confiscated food stores outside of Jerusalem. When Nebuchadnezzar surrounded Jerusalem with his army, the land began to enjoy its overdue rest. There would be no planting or harvesting for the next seventy years.

One may wonder why the Lord would impose a seventy-year cessation from agricultural work. The Mosaic Law commanded that the Sabbath Day be set aside to rest and to honor God. The Jews, their slaves, and their beasts of burden were all to rest on the Sabbath Day. Likewise, the Israelites were to honor a Sabbath Year. Every seventh year, the fields, the olive groves, and the vineyards were to receive a full year's rest. Whatever grew naturally during this time was to be freely gleaned by the poor, and anything left would be God's provision for the beasts of the field. The Sabbatical Year was to remind the Jews that God owned the land they dwelled upon and that they were merely stewards of it (Lev. 25:23).

This was God's Law for the land. Unfortunately, the Jews often ignored the Sabbath Year. According to 2 Chronicles 36:14-21, the reason for the specific length of time was that exactly seventy years were due to the Lord as His portion (i.e., one-seventh of the 490 years the Jews did not honor the Sabbath Year). This judgment began on December 13, 589 BC. and ended, according to the prophet Haggai, when the foundation of the temple was laid on the base previously completed. Like Ezekiel, Haggai recorded the exact day that the Lord lifted the forced agricultural rest:

Consider now from this day forward, from the twenty-fourth day of the ninth month, from the day that the foundation of the Lord's temple was laid – consider it: Is the seed still in the barn? As yet the vine, the fig tree, the pomegranate, and the olive tree have not yielded fruit. But from this day I will bless you (Hag. 2:18-19).

The Jews who had returned from Babylon and had just laid the foundation of the second temple were to enjoy the benefits of the land again. This occurred on December 17, 520 BC. It is significant that Haggai prophesied that the Jewish Messiah would one day stand in the temple being constructed and offer peace (Hag. 2:6-9). That temple was completed in 516 BC and destroyed in AD 70, which means the Jewish Messiah must have stood in that temple sometime in that time period.

Indeed, the Gospels record that the Lord Jesus presented Himself in this temple and offered a message of peace.

To validate the fulfillment of Jeremiah's seventy-year agricultural prophecy, God caused Ezekiel to record the exact starting date of its fulfillment and caused Haggai to record the precise ending date. A Jewish year is 360 days (Rev. 12:6, 14; 13:5; Dan. 12:7) meaning that there are 25,200 days in 70 Jewish years (i.e., 70 x 360 days = 25,200 days). Thus, as Sir Robert Anderson confirms in the tenth edition of *The Coming Prince*, the seventy-year period of rest that started on December 13, 589 BC. ended on December 17, 520 BC., the exact day that God restored the land to fruitfulness according to Haggai.[1] The land enjoyed seventy years of sabbatical rest to the exact day, to prove again that God's Word stands sure for all time. Just as Jeremiah predicted, the Jews were captives in Babylon for seventy years and the land also experienced seventy years of agricultural rest.

Daniel's Seventy-Week Prophecy

Just as Jeremiah's two seventy-year prophecies provided the timetable for the end of Jewish exile in Babylon and the renewal of agricultural blessing in Israel, God moved Daniel to declare His ultimate timetable for the final restoration of the Jewish nation. Daniel's seventy-week prophecy reads as follows (Dan. 9:24-27):

Know therefore and understand, that from the going forth of the command to restore and build Jerusalem until Messiah the Prince, there shall be seven weeks and sixty-two weeks; the street shall be built again, and the wall, even in troublesome times. And after the sixty-two weeks Messiah shall be cut off, but not for Himself; and the people of the prince who is to come shall destroy the city and the sanctuary. The end of it shall be with a flood, and till the end of the war desolations are determined. Then he shall confirm a covenant with many for one week; but in the middle of the week he shall bring an end to sacrifice and offering and on the wing of abominations shall be one who makes desolate, even until the consummation, which is determined, is poured out on the desolate.

The prophecy is broken into two major parts: sixty-nine weeks, which consists of two portions of seven weeks and sixty-two weeks, and then the final section of one week. The word translated "week" is literally "seven." But seven what? Based on how the final week is described elsewhere in Scripture, we are able to conclude that a week is speaking of seven years. The abomination of desolation committed by the Antichrist (the one who will make a peace covenant with the Jewish nation for one week) occurs in the middle of the week (Dan. 8:25; 9:27; Matt. 24:15; 2 Thess. 2:4). But Scripture elsewhere provides the exact timing of this event. It occurs "a time (1), times (2), and half a time (1/2)" after the start of the week of years (Dan. 7:25; 12:7; Rev. 12:14). This three and a half times is also equal to 1260 days (Rev. 12:6) or 42 months (Rev. 13:5). As just witnessed in the fulfillment of Jeremiah's seventy-year prophecy, a Jewish prophetic year in Scripture is consistently 360 days (12 months x 30 days/month = 360 days). Three and a half years would then be equal to 1260 days (3.5 years x 360 days/year = 1260 days). Thus, Daniel's prophecy is unmistakably speaking of seventy weeks of years or, literally, "seventy sevens."

Only Calvary could be referred to by the phrases *"to make an end of sin"* and *"to make reconciliation for iniquity."* The passage is thus Messianic in nature since it speaks of Christ being cut off and also establishing everlasting righteousness among His people. Daniel's first sixty-nine weeks of years (or 173,880 days) span the time from the command to rebuild Jerusalem (given to Nehemiah by Persian king Artaxeres Longimanus) to the time of Christ's death ("Messiah shall be cut off"). Included in this time period were the seven sevens or forty-nine years to fully rebuild the walls and the city of Jerusalem (i.e., in fifth century BC).

It is obvious that this prophetic clock pertaining to the Jews stopped temporarily after their Messiah was cut off. The evidence for this is within the prophecy itself. The destruction of Jerusalem by the Romans occurred in AD 70, some thirty-eight years after Messiah was cut off, yet there is only one week (seven years) left in the prophecy after the death of Messiah. Also, the prophecy speaks of the destruction of Jerusalem as occurring after the cutting off of Messiah but before Antichrist's covenant with Israel. When Israel rejected her Messiah, her prophetic clock was temporarily stopped. Once the Antichrist signs the peace treaty with Israel, the prophetic clock will begin its final seven-year countdown and the Tribulation Period will start.

Both the starting point and the ending point of Daniel's prophecy are fixed. There would be sixty-nine weeks of years or 173,880 days (69 weeks x 7 years/week x 360 days/Jewish year = 173,880 days) from the command of Artaxerxes Longimanus to Nehemiah to rebuild the wall about Jerusalem (March 14, 445 BC) until Messiah's final presentation in Jerusalem (April 6, AD 32) and subsequent death.[2] The exact date will vary depending on the chronology used to date the rebuilding command. But like Jeremiah's seventy-week prophecies, the sixty-nine week portion of Daniel's prophecy has been precisely fulfilled. The final week, associated with the Jewish nation, will begin with the signing of a covenant with the Antichrist. The following diagram provides an overview of major prophetic events in relationship to Daniel's seventy-week prophecy.

BIBLE PROPHECY OVERVIEW

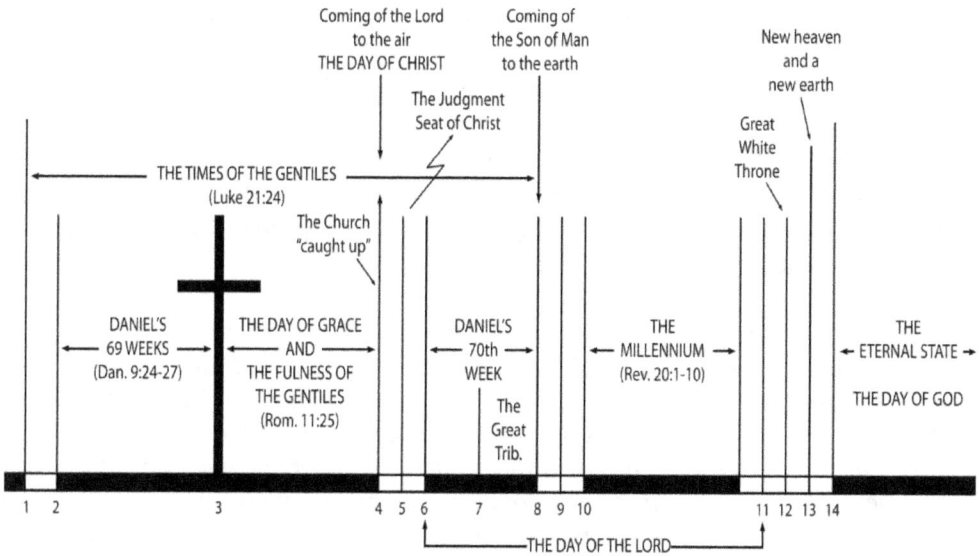

1. The Times of the Gentiles (Jer. 25:1)
2. Decree to rebuild Jerusalem (Neh. 2:1-8)
3. The cross of our Lord Jesus Christ (Luke 23:33)
4. The coming of the Lord to the air (1 Thess. 4:16-17)
5. The Judgment Seat of Christ (2 Cor. 5:10)
6. The 70th week of Daniel's prophecy (Dan. 9:26-27)
7. The Great Tribulation (Matt. 24:21)
8. The coming of the Son of Man (2 Thess. 2:7-8; Matt. 24:30)
9. The judgment of the living nations (Matt. 25:31-33)
10. The Millennium (Rev. 20:4-6)
11. The final rebellion (Rev. 20:7-9)
12. The judgment of the Great White Throne (Rev. 20:11-15)
13. The new heaven and the new earth (Rev. 21:1-5)
14. The eternal state (2 Pet. 1:11; 3:11-12)

The Predicted Jewish Regathering

Prophesies predicting a Jewish regathering to the land of Israel, such as Isaiah 11:12 and Ezekiel 39:28-29, are not yet complete. Ezra and Nehemiah record that many dispersed Jews from the southern kingdom of Judah did return from Babylon to Israel in the fifth and sixth centuries BC, exactly as Jeremiah prophesied years earlier. However, most of the northern ten nations have not returned to the land yet, nor have all of the Jews from the southern kingdom returned to Israel! Accordingly, Jeremiah's prophecy pertaining to the broader event remains unrealized:

> *In those days the house of Judah shall walk with the house of Israel, and they shall come together out of the land of the north to the land that I have given as an inheritance to your fathers. But I said: "How can I put you among the children and give you a pleasant land, a beautiful heritage of the hosts of nations?" And I said: "You shall call Me, 'My Father,' and not turn away from Me. Surely, as a wife treacherously departs from her husband, so have you dealt treacherously with Me, O house of Israel," says the Lord* (Jer. 3:18-20).

Judah and Israel have not yet fully returned to the land, nor have they come together to worship the Messiah. During Judah's Babylonian captivity, Jehovah prompted the prophet Ezekiel to provide more detail as to when these events would occur.

> *Again the word of the Lord came to me, saying, "As for you, son of man, take a stick for yourself and write on it: 'For **Judah** and for the children of Israel, his companions.' Then take another stick and write on it, 'For Joseph, the stick of Ephraim, and for all the house of **Israel**, his companions.' Then join them one to another for yourself into one stick, and they will become one in your hand. And when the children of your people speak to you, saying, 'Will you not show us what you mean by these?' – Say to them, 'Thus says the Lord God: "Surely I will take the stick of Joseph, which is in the hand of Ephraim, and the tribes of Israel, his companions; and I will join them with it, with the stick of Judah, and make them one stick, and they will be one in My hand."' And the sticks on which you write will be in your hand before their eyes. Then say to them, 'Thus says the Lord God: "Surely I will take the children of Israel from among the nations, wherever*

34

they have gone, and will gather them from every side and bring them into their own land; and I will make them one nation in the land, on the mountains of Israel; and one king shall be king over them all; **they shall no longer be two nations**, *nor shall they ever be divided into two kingdoms again. They shall not defile themselves any more with their idols, nor with their detestable things, nor with any of their transgressions; but I will deliver them from all their dwelling places in which they have sinned, and will cleanse them. Then they shall be My people, and I will be their God"'"* (37:15-23).

Ezekiel states that when the Lord begins to bring His people back into the Promised Land from among the nations, there will not be two political realities as before (i.e., a northern kingdom, Israel, or a southern kingdom, Judah). The prophet symbolized this truth by taking two sticks and making them one, which would be called "Israel" (Ezek. 37:28), the name God gave to Jacob, the father of the nation (Gen. 32:28). This would mean, as Ezekiel goes on to explain, that two kings would not reign over His people, but one king, the promised Messiah from the line of David, would rule the nation:

David My servant shall be king over them, and they shall all have one shepherd; they shall also walk in My judgments and observe My statutes, and do them. Then they shall dwell in the land that I have given to Jacob My servant, where your fathers dwelt; and they shall dwell there, they, their children, and their children's children, forever; and My servant David shall be their prince forever. Moreover I will make a covenant of peace with them, and it shall be an everlasting covenant with them; I will establish them and multiply them, and I will set My sanctuary in their midst forevermore. My tabernacle also shall be with them; indeed I will be their God, and they shall be My people. The nations also will know that I, the Lord, sanctify Israel, when My sanctuary is in their midst forevermore (Ezek. 37:15-28).

Obviously, the Jews are not completely back in the Promised Land, worshipping their Messiah in a sanctuary set up by Him. Neither do the nations honor Christ or esteem the nation of Israel. Jeremiah's seventy-year prophesy has been fulfilled and many Jews did return from Babylon to Judah. But Ezekiel foretold that by the end of the Tribulation

Period, every Jew remaining among the nations will be physically brought back to dwell in the land of Israel (Ezek. 39:28-29).

Isaiah, Jeremiah, and Ezekiel all prophesied that in a future day, Judah and Israel will no longer be two nations, but one. This will happen when they come into their inheritance in Christ's Kingdom. Ezekiel added that when the Jewish nation is restored, it will be called "Israel." These prophecies refer to God's dealings with the Jews just prior to and then during the millennial kingdom, when Christ will rule over them as their king (Ezek. 37:22). Consequently, as we approach the end of the Church Age, the initiation of these prophecies will be apparent, especially the regathering of Jews back into the land of Israel after centuries of global exile.

Bible prophecy is in motion, Israel has become a Jewish nation again, but God's covenant people are yet to be fully regathered to the land promised to Abraham (Gen. 15:18-21). The boundaries of this inheritance were confirmed when the Israelites entered Canaan under Joshua's leadership (Josh. 1:3-4). The Jews have yet to possess this vast region of land, which means that if God is a covenant-keeping God, He is not done with the Jewish nation yet. The seventieth week of Daniel's prophecy is rapidly approaching; at that time, the Lord will spiritually refine His people and physically restore them to the land promised to Abraham's descendants through Jacob.

Bible Prophecy in Motion

Would you believe someone who warned you of a specific danger to avoid tomorrow, if that person had previously and correctly foretold hundreds of specific events in your future without error? Statistically speaking, such a feat defies the laws of natural order and indicates some type of supernatural influence. While Satan does mimic God's handiwork and does deceive mankind through supernatural signs, he cannot explicitly control future events or create life (Ex. 8:16-19), nor is he omniscient, knowing the end from the beginning. Only God can forecast and govern forthcoming events with precise accuracy.

Isaiah explained to his fellow countrymen that this was why much of God's messages to them was prophetic in nature – He wanted them to know He was the one true God so they would reject the many false gods of their day. *"Even from the beginning I have declared it to you; before it came to pass I proclaimed it to you, lest you should say, 'My idol has done them, and my carved image and my molded image have commanded them'"* (Isa. 48:5). Only the true Creator and Sustainer of all things could possibly know what will transpire in the future – Jehovah was proving to His people that He was the omnipotent, omniscient, immutable, and eternal God. This is why the far majority of prophetic content in the Bible relates to God's covenant people – Jehovah wanted the Jews to flee idolatry and embrace Him, the one true God.

Unfortunately, false prophets have plagued the Jews throughout their history. The problem is compounded by the fact that God's prophets always seemed to be greatly outnumbered at any given time by their counterparts. The ministries of Elijah (1 Kings 18), Micaiah (1 Kings 22), and Jeremiah (Jer. 20) serve as good examples. All of this goes to say that, time and again, God's prophets have suffered greatly for their faithfulness to be one voice for God among a throng of dissident and often hostile people. The standard of a true prophet of God is one hundred percent accuracy (Deut. 18:20-22). This provides confirmation that the message is indeed from God.

Thankfully, we have the Old Testament writings, including prophecy, to study and to appreciate. It is my firmest belief that God will not restart Israel's prophetic clock until after Christ has returned to the air to remove His Church from the earth (Rom. 11:25; 1 Cor. 15:51-52; 1 Thess. 4:13-18). No believer, having trusted Christ and experienced regeneration, will experience God's wrath for sin (Rom. 5:8; 1 Thess. 1:10; 1 Thess. 5:9). On the cross, Christ was made sin for us; God the Father punished His Son for our offenses, that we might be forgiven and obtain a righteous standing before Him and escape judgment (2 Cor. 5:21; Col. 2:12; 1 Tim. 2:5-6). Thus, Paul said all Christians who live expectantly in light of Christ's imminent return will receive a reward, a crown of righteousness, at the Judgment Seat of Christ (2 Tim. 4:8).

With this understanding, believers today should be excited about a number of recent events which seemingly indicate that after centuries of exile, God has begun the process of restoring the Jewish nation in the land of Israel. These foretold signs indicate that Israel's spiritual renewal is nearing.

The Jews Back in Palestine

On May 14, 1948, while Egyptian fighter-bombers flew overhead and the last remaining British troops prepared to depart Palestine, Ben Gurion and his cabinet gathered at the Tel Aviv Museum where they proclaimed the independence of the state of Israel. After almost 2,600 years of being a dispersed people scattered throughout the world, the miracle rebirth of the Jewish nation occurred. Considering most conquered or displaced people simply blend into the fabric of the society that is forced upon them, the fact that the Jews maintained their distinction as God's covenant people for all that time is miraculous.

As delineated in the previous chapter, the Lord has promised to bring the Jews back to their homeland from all nations. The prophecies of Isaiah, Jeremiah, and Ezekiel do not pertain merely to the return of Jews from their Babylonian or Assyrian exiles; these have a far broader application. The prophet Ezekiel precisely identified when this promise would be fulfilled as being after the battle of Gog and Magog near the end of the first half of the Tribulation Period (Ezek. 38:1-39:12). At that time, Israel will be back in their land and resting from warfare (Ezek. 38:8).

Statistical analysis confirms that the process of gathering Jews back to Zion began in the early twentieth century. All Jews will be dwelling with their Messiah in Israel at the end of the Tribulation Period (Ezek. 39:28-29). The following chart shows the percentage of Jews world-wide that have returned to the land of Israel in recent years:

Year	Percent of Jews Worldwide Back in Israel[1]
1882	0
1900	1
1925	1
1939	3
1948	6
1955	13
1970	20
1980	25
1990	30
2000	37
2010	42
2012	43

In March 2012, the Israeli Census Bureau of Statistics forecasted that in 2019, Israel will be home to 6,940,000 Jews.[2] If this projection is correct, that would mean that half of the world's Jewish population will reside in the land of Israel. In January 2013, it was reported by the Jerusalem Post that the population of Israeli Jews is expected to reach between 7.4 to 9.3 million by the year 2035.[3]

Palestine became a Jewish state again in May 1948, a situation that was immediately and violently challenged by surrounding Arab countries. The land belonging to the Jewish state was further expanded after their victory in the Six-Day War of 1967. Furthermore, Israel's national sovereignty has been repeatedly challenged by war, yet Israel has emerged victorious in each situation. This is exactly what was prophesied through Ezekiel: the Jews would be dispersed because of idolatry

(Ezek. 38:17-19), gathered back out of the nations in a future day (Ezek. 38:24), and back in the land of Israel (Ezek. 38:8).

Suddenly a Nation

As explained in the previous chapter, the Bible states that the Jewish people, when restored to the land of Israel, will not be two political realities (Judah in the south and Israel in the north) but one unified nation. The prophet Isaiah foretold that the Jewish nation, Israel, would be reborn in a day and all the nations would marvel at the event:

Who has ever heard of such a thing? Who has ever seen such things? Can a country be born in a day or a nation be brought forth in a moment? Yet no sooner is Zion in labor than she gives birth to her children (Isa. 66:8 NIV).

Israel, as a self-governing nation, did not exist from 605 BC to AD 1948. But on May 14, 1948, the United States recognized Israel's national sovereignty, as did the USSR three days later. Nineteen other countries also recognized Israel's statehood before the end of 1948 and another twelve did in 1949. The nation of Israel was born in a day. On May 15, 1948, the armies of Egypt, Transjordan, Iraq, Syria, and Lebanon invaded Israel and the War of Independence began. Israel, immensely outnumbered and outgunned, emerged victorious, but not without great cost. Thousands of Israeli and Arab soldiers died and approximately 600,000 Palestinians fled their homes, thus creating a "refugee problem" that continues to trouble the region to this day.[4] Isaiah prophesied that the nations would marvel that such a feat could happen in a day and that this event would occur shortly before the initiation of Christ's millennial kingdom (Isa. 66:10-18). The United Nations recognized Israel as a sovereign state the following year by a majority vote.

The Order of the Jewish Return

The order in which the Jews would return to Palestine is also prophetically predicted in Psalm 107:2-3 and Isaiah 43:5-6; the latter reads as follows:

Fear not, for I am with you; I will bring your descendants from the east, and gather you from the west; I will say to the north, "Give them up!" and to the south, "Do not keep them back!" Bring My sons from afar, and My daughters from the ends of the earth.

The precise order of return set forth in this verse (from the east, west, north, and then south) is reflected in recent history. The first wave of Jews to return to Palestine came from the eastern Arab countries. For example, *Operation Magic Carpet* brought 49,000 Yemenite Jews to the new state of Israel from June 1949 to September 1950. British and American transport planes made some 380 flights from Aden in a secret operation to bring these Jews home. The second wave came from Western Europe, especially Germany. The third wave came from Russia (the north) during the 1980s to early 1990s; nearly one million Jews returned to Israel during this period. The fourth wave of Jews returning to Israel came most recently from Ethiopia (the south).

Even today, there are secret operations to return Jews from hostile countries to Israel. For example, the *Jewish Journal* recently reported that seventeen Yemeni Jews had been airlifted to Israel in a covert operation:

Four of the Jews were flown directly from Yemen to Israel's Ben Gurion Airport on Wednesday, Haaretz reported. The rest were taken clandestinely from Buenos Aires after being smuggled to the Argentinian capital by a group of Satmar hasidim in August 2011, living in the Satmar community there. The Satmars have been involved in smuggling Jews out of Yemen for several years, according to Haaretz. Several of the Yemenis reunited with family members in Israel. The operation – a coordinated effort among the Jewish Agency and the Israeli ministries for the interior, foreign affairs and immigration absorption was prompted by growing concern for the safety of the Jews in Yemen, according to the Jewish Agency. Anti-Semitic violence has been a growing problem since the 2011 ouster of President Ali Abdullah Saleh. The airlift brings to 45 the number of Yemeni Jews who have been brought to Israel this year and 151 since 2009. Fewer than 90 Jews remain in Yemen, with about half of them living in a guarded structure in the capital.[5]

The growing Anti-Semitism around the world is resulting in increased Jewish immigration back to their homeland. Jehovah has begun to bring His covenant people back to Israel and He is doing so just as Isaiah prophesied in the eighth century BC.

Back in Bashan

An important prediction by the prophet Jeremiah refines our understanding of when the nation of Israel will experience spiritual renewal – at the time when the Lord intervenes to protect the already existing nation, whose capital is Jerusalem (Zech. 14:2) from Babylon:

> *But I will bring back Israel to his home, and he shall feed on Carmel and Bashan; his soul shall be satisfied on Mount Ephraim and Gilead. In those days and in that time," says the Lord, "the iniquity of Israel shall be sought, but there shall be none; and the sins of Judah, but they shall not be found; for I will pardon those whom I preserve* (Jer. 50:19-21).

The verses following this prophecy detail the utter destruction of Babylon by the Lord to protect His people, the Jews. Directly following this event they will receive Jesus as Christ and His forgiveness (Ezek. 36:24-27; Zech. 12:8-10). The destruction of Babylon is more thoroughly discussed in a later chapter; it suffices here to acknowledge that Jeremiah foretold that Israel would regain Bashan as a possession. Bashan (the Golan Heights in northeastern Israel) did not become a Jewish possession until after the Six Day War of 1967. The fact that Israel is back in Bashan after not possessing that region for nearly 2,600 years suggests that the spiritual rebirth of the Jewish nation is fast approaching.

Restored Cities in Israel

As the ancient nation was being destroyed by Babylon, Ezekiel foretold that many of these destroyed cities would, in fact, be rebuilt and re-settled in the exact same locations after the Jewish exile was complete:

And I will multiply upon you man and beast; and they shall increase and bring fruit: and I will settle you after your old estates, and will do better [unto you] than at your beginnings: and ye shall know that I [am] the Lord.... For I will take you from among the heathen, and gather you out of all countries, and will bring you into your own land (Ezek. 36:11; 24).

Today, there are many cities in Israel that bear the ancient names of previous biblical cities: Cana, Nazareth, Jericho, Nain, Bethany, Bethlehem, Hebron, Gaza, etc. Ezekiel's prophecy has been fulfilled. It is also noted that the Lord Jesus put a curse on some Jewish cities such as Capernaum, Bethsaida, and Chorazin for their rejection of His message (Luke 10:13-16). Only a few ancient ruins remain of those Jewish cities today. Several cities in Israel today are called by their ancient names; however, those specifically cursed by Christ do not exist.

Agricultural Renewal

Another event that Scripture prophesied would identify God's blessing upon the new nation of Israel is that they would become an agricultural icon in the world. Isaiah not only speaks of this achievement, but also associates the timing of this realization to when Jehovah gathers His people out of the nations to worship Him in Jerusalem (Isa. 27:13). Though the Jewish nation has not fully returned to Israel, nor do they yet worship their Messiah, the process of gathering them back "one by one" has begun (Isa. 27:12). Isaiah writes:

Those who come He shall cause to take root in Jacob; Israel shall blossom and bud, and fill the face of the world with fruit (Isa. 27:6).

The wilderness and the wasteland shall be glad for them, and the desert shall rejoice and blossom as the rose (Isa. 35:1).

The agricultural prosperity of Israel today, including the flourishing forests there, has been another remarkable miracle. Seventy-five years ago, Israel was full of malarial swamps and deserts. Today, the replanted forests are thriving and the Israeli agricultural production is amazing. John Fedler, editor of *Agritech Israel Magazine,* summarizes what has been accomplished.

43

When Jews began resettling their historic homeland in the late 19th century, their first efforts were directed towards reclaiming the mostly semi-arid land, much of which was rendered untillable by deforestation, soil erosion and neglect. Rocky fields were cleared and terraces built in the hilly regions; swampland was drained, and systematic reforestation begun; soil erosion was counteracted, and salty land washed to reduce soil salinity.

Since Israel attained its independence in 1948, the total area under cultivation has increased from 165,000 ha. to some 435,000 ha. and the number of agricultural communities has grown from 400 to 900 (including 136 Arab villages). During the same period, agricultural production has expanded 16-fold, more than three times the rate of the population growth.

Israel's varied climatic, topographical and soil conditions (from subtropical to arid, from 400 meters below sea level to 1000 meters above and from sand dunes to heavy alluvial soils) made it possible to grow a wide range of agricultural produce. The success of the country's agriculture stems from the determination and ingenuity of farmers and scientists who have dedicated themselves to developing a flourishing agriculture in a country which is more than half desert, thus demonstrating that the real value of land is a function of how it is used.[6]

From 1950 to 1984, the amount of irrigated land in Israel increased from fifteen to fifty-four percent and agricultural production has expanded sixteen-fold (more than three times the rate of the population growth). Today, there are farms in Israel that are bearing three and four bountiful crops a year. After centuries of being mostly unproductive, Israel has become an agricultural marvel.

The Shekel Restored

Ezekiel foretold that after Israel became a political reality again they would have their own currency and it would be the same as used in Old Testament days, the shekel:

The shekel is to consist of twenty gerahs. Twenty shekels plus twenty-five shekels plus fifteen shekels equal one mina.... All the people of the land will participate in this special gift for the use of the prince in Israel (Ezek. 45:12-16).

Although the context of this Scripture refers to the Millennial Kingdom, it is quite interesting that after almost 2,000 years the shekel has been reinstated as the common monetary unit in Israel, just as predicted by Ezekiel.

Summary

Israel's sudden political re-establishment, present agricultural prosperity, reinstated national currency, and restored cities were all predicted over two millennia ago. Even the order in which God would retrieve His people back to Palestine and what cities and lands they would occupy after returning was foretold and has been witnessed. Jehovah is doing exactly what He said He would do so that the Jews, and mankind in general, might know that He is the one true God. This is the reason that the "holy books" of world religions are nearly void of prophecy. The devil does not know and cannot control the future. But time does not constrain the Creator; instead, He honors Himself by working His revealed will in time so that we might know that He is the true and living God.

The Bible has much to say about future events. Fulfilled prophecy is one of the evidences that the Bible is indeed God's Word to humanity. The prophecies just mentioned, as well as others, relate to the restoration of the Jewish nation to Jehovah. These are exciting times; we are seeing God's Word being fulfilled before our eyes and there are many more significant events peeking over the prophetic horizon. God is a promise-keeping God and, by His everlasting love, He is drawing His covenant people into His sovereign purposes for them. Their ultimate oneness with God will establish them in everlasting peace.

Impending Predictions

Sunrises occur so frequently that we often do not appreciate their beauty. Yet, if you were waiting out the night alone in the still blackness of a vast forest or a tropical jungle, you would have a much deeper appreciation for those first hues of morning bliss creeping over the eastern horizon. This is why Christ, in the closing passage of Scripture, likens Himself to *"the bright and morning star"* (Rev. 22:16) which is most noticeable in the eastern sky just before dawn. Focusing on Christ instead of the spiritual darkness we are living in inspires hope for the glorious day which is to come. For this reason, John writes, *"For the testimony of Jesus is the spirit of prophecy"* (Rev. 19:10). Bible prophecy is centered in the person of Jesus Christ, the Bright and Morning Star. Scripture contains predawn events of His coming in order to encourage those who are watching and waiting for Him. Consider two examples.

In his first epistle, Paul had spoken of Christ's imminent coming for His Church (1 Thess. 4:13-18) and also of the Day of the Lord which would follow (1 Thess. 5:1-5). Shortly after receiving Paul's first epistle, someone, apparently posing as the Apostle Paul, wrote a letter to discourage the church at Thessalonica (2 Thess. 2:2). These new and persecuted believers were wrongly informed by the counterfeit letter that they had missed the coming of Christ and were now in the Day of the Lord. Paul wrote his second epistle to the Thessalonian believers in order to correct the erroneous teaching.

Paul's main emphasis was to affirm that they were not in the Tribulation Period, since Christ had not yet returned to remove the Church from the earth. He then described two things that must happen prior to the commencement of the Day of the Lord: the professing Church will become apostate and the Man of Sin, the Antichrist, will be revealed (2 Thess. 2:3-6). Dark times will precede the curtain call of the Church Age, yet believers have the hope of their *Bright and Morning Star*. He shall come for His beloved bride at the dawning of the Day of the Lord, and then the *Sun of Righteousness* (Mal. 4:2) shall rise in His full fury and flood the earth with His glory!

Likewise, after delivering his thirteen prophetic messages to rebellious Judah, the Spirit of God moved Jeremiah to weave a lovely interlude of hope and deliverance. The content of this is recorded in Jeremiah 30-33. This portion of Scripture contains a twofold prophecy pertaining to the Jews' return from Babylonian exile. The first part of the prophecy was fulfilled in the sixth century BC; the latter portion relates to their future and final national restoration with God. In this section of the text, the near-term (predawn) restoration of the Jewish nation was spoken of as *"the days are coming"* (Jer. 30:3). Jews in subsequent centuries would understand that Jehovah had kept the predawn sign of the coming day and be encouraged during the intense suffering that He would also fulfill the rest of the prophecy. Jeremiah likens this Jewish situation to a woman giving birth – pain before joy (Jer. 30:6).

Their final restoration, referred to as "that day" – a great day the like of which never was (Jer. 30:8) would be preceded by a period of intense suffering called *"the time of Jacob's trouble"* (Jer. 30:7). Most of the unfulfilled Bible prophecies pertaining to the Jewish nation of Israel focus on this timeframe. Many current events, as discussed in the previous chapter, indicate that the time of Jacob's trouble, the Tribulation Period, is rapidly approaching. With this understanding, what does Scripture say will be the next events to unfold for the nation of Israel? Are there any more predawn signs? The following is a list of the most prevalent and anticipated events:

Revival of the Old Roman Empire

According to the prophet Daniel (writing in sixth century BC), there would be five world empires after the Egyptian and Assyrian empires. The Babylonian empire was ruling in Daniel's day and would be followed by the Medo-Persian, Greek, Roman, and Revived Roman empires (Dan. 2, 7-9). These various world systems in which Satan has reigned or will reign are depicted in the seven heads of two beasts described by John in the book of Revelation:

- A terrible red dragon having seven heads, ten horns, and seven crowns (one for each of its heads) is used to represent Satan (Rev. 12:3). He is identified as Satan, the devil, and the serpent of old (Rev. 12:9).
- A beast rising up out of the sea (i.e., the nations) with seven heads and ten horns on one head with each horn having a crown represents the Antichrist who speaks for the dragon (Rev. 13:1, 17:9-14).
- A beast coming up out of the land (i.e., Israel) and having two horns, like a lamb, represents the false prophet who talks like the dragon (Rev. 13:11).

These beasts form an unholy trio that clearly mocks the Holy Trinity in form and operation: God the Father directs, the Son does the Father's will, and the Holy Spirit enables the Son to do the Father's will. Satan directs the affairs of the unholy trio. The Antichrist is the devil's human representative on earth and does his will. The false prophet gives honor to the beast through miracles and deceives many into worshiping the beast, and thus honoring Satan (Rev. 13:14-15). These similarities between the unholy trio and the Holy Trinity are profound.

John again describes the Antichrist in Revelation 17 and there identifies the heads of the beast as being kingdoms. At the time of John's writing, approximately AD 95, five of these kingdoms had fallen: the Egyptian, the Assyrian, the Babylonian, the Medo-Persian, and the Greek empires. The sixth kingdom, the Roman Empire, ruled in John's day. One world government had yet to be established, but Daniel identifies it as a Revived Roman Empire in which the Antichrist would rule with ten kings initially and then with seven (Dan. 8:8, 24; Rev. 17:9-14). Human history has shown Daniel's prophecy to be true thus far. Though many nations have tried, there has not been a world empire since the fall of Roman rule in the fifth century AD.

Daniel precisely named the Medo-Persian and then the Greek empires long before they were established (Dan. 8:20-21). Understanding that the heads of the beasts represent kingdoms, and that the horns represent kings within the final kingdom explains why the crowns were on each of the seven heads of the dragon (depicting Satan's control of seven world empires), but were only on the ten horns of the seventh head, the final empire, when speaking of the beast rising out of the sea, the

Antichrist. Paul identifies Satan as *"the god of this age"* (2 Cor. 4:4), and *"the prince of the power of the air"* (Eph. 2:2). On three occasions, the Lord Jesus said that Satan is *"the prince of this world"* (John 12:31, 14:30, 16:11). The world is presently Satan's delegated domain; he is the ruler of all seven world empires that span time leading up to the reign of Christ.

The revived Roman empire must be in place prior to the abomination of desolation which occurs at the midpoint in the Tribulation Period, since that is when the harlot, the one-world religious system, is destroyed by the Antichrist (Rev. 17:16). Is this world empire established today? No, there is no one world economic or political system centered in the old Roman empire which governs the world. But do we see this dominating system forming?

Consider that for 1600 years there has not been a world empire and the old Roman empire has shown no signs of reasserting itself until the twentieth century. Europe was decimated by WW2, but the 1957 Treaty of Rome unified six war-torn nations: Belgium, France, Italy, Luxembourg, the Netherlands, and West Germany, and established the European Economic Community (EEC). The first enlargement was in 1973, with the accession of Denmark, Ireland, and the United Kingdom. Greece, Spain, and Portugal joined throughout the 1980s. Following the creation of the EU in 1993, it has enlarged to include a further sixteen countries. On July 1, 2013, Croatia became the twenty-eighth member of the EU.

What is the present economic power of the European Union? The World Bank reported that the U.S. Gross National Product (GNP) was $15.7 trillion in 2012 and the EU GNP was $16.7 trillion for that same year.[1] The United States presently has the greatest economic strength of any single country on earth, but as a united entity, the European Union has surpassed the U.S. GNP for the past several years. In just a little over sixty years, a handful of war-torn countries have unified to become the world's strongest economic power. This is an economic reality that has not been witnessed in a united Europe for sixteen hundred years. Is the revived Roman empire predicted by the Bible being established? It certainly will be at the time the Antichrist signs a peace treaty with the nation of Israel and is permitted to reign over the planet.

Levitical Sacrifices Restored

The Jewish nation is allegorically likened to a foliage trilogy: the vine, the fig tree, and the olive tree. Each one represents a distinct aspect of the nation's existence. For example, the prophet Jeremiah, told his fellow countrymen that God had planted a beautiful vineyard (Israel), but Israel's shepherds had made it desolate (Jer. 12:10). The nation of Israel, as a political reality, is likened to a noble vine (a grape vine; Jer. 8:13), which God planted in the world (Jer. 2:21; 12:10); Israel was God's vineyard. Jeremiah explains that the destruction of Israel in his day would be like livestock moving freely through God's vineyard and trampling the vines. It would consequently have no productivity, bearing only the fruit of sowing to sin, that is, the thorns of affliction and a harvest of shame (Jer. 12:11-13).

When Israel is spoken of as a fig tree in Scripture, the metaphor relates to the religious element of Israel, which often was fruitless for God (Jer. 8:13; Matt. 21:19-21). This reality, Judaism today, was identified during one of the events in the life of the Lord Jesus (Luke 13:6-9). After preaching three years to the lost nation of Israel, Christ cursed the fruitless fig tree just before His death at Calvary. Less than forty years later, Jerusalem and the temple were destroyed and the Jews have not sacrificed since then. The Old Covenant was replaced by the New Covenant, sealed with Christ's blood, and God was determined not to allow the Jews to continue in what was now obsolete.

One of the signs that the Tribulation Period and the Second Advent of Christ are nearing is that the fig tree (i.e., religious Israel) will again shoot forth leaves after a long winter season of deadness (Luke 21:29-31). Leaves must precede fruit, but the fig tree will bear no fruit until the rebirth of the nation occurs in the latter days of the Tribulation Period. What might the new leaves speak of? This is likely a reference to the Jews reviving the old sacrificial system during, and perhaps just prior to, the Tribulation Period.

We know from various prophecies that the Antichrist will desecrate the Jewish temple and put a stop to animal sacrifices at the midpoint of the Tribulation Period (Dan. 9:27; Matt. 24:15; 2 Thess. 2:3-7). Therefore, logically speaking, a temple will have to be erected and animal sacrifices will have to be reinstituted by that point.

Therefore, we see that, during the Tribulation Period, the Jews will again offer sacrifices under the Levitical system. This reality could commence just prior to the Tribulation period. The Lord Jesus said that the generation permitted to witness this event would also visibly see His coming to the earth in glory (Luke 21:32). It is worth noting that the Temple Institute in Jerusalem has already recreated most of the temple vessels and furnishing and has actually performed "educational" animal sacrifices in anticipation of this historic event.

> Rabbi Yisrael Ariel, one of the leaders of the Temple Institute in Jerusalem, has stated that everything is now ready for recommencement of the sacrificial system. All that remains is for the government of Israel to give them the permission to go onto the Temple Mount and perform the sacrifice. While Israel does control the Temple Mount, it is administered by the Islamic Waqf of Jordan, and the Israeli Police generally prohibit any action that might cause contention with the Muslims.[2]

Certainly, many orthodox Jews are anticipating an imminent day when they will again perform the sacrifices as specified in the Mosaic Law.

At this juncture, there are leaves upon the tree, depicting a religious reality, but there is no fruit. Spiritual fruit can only be produced through spiritual rebirth which coincides with the Holy Spirit being poured out upon the Jewish nation at the end of the Tribulation Period. At that time, they will know and worship Jesus Christ as Messiah (Joel 2:25-3:21; Zech. 12:10-13:1). At the end of the Tribulation Period, the refined Jewish nation will receive the Holy Spirit and obtain spiritual life in Christ – this is depicted by the olive tree and will be discussed momentarily. Once the Jewish nation has experienced spiritual renewal, the vineyard of the Lord (i.e., the house of Israel; Isa. 5:7) will be again planted in Israel as a testimony to the nations of God's glory (Isa. 4; 60:1-5).

Jews Dwelling Safely in Israel

At the beginning of the Tribulation Period the Jews will be back in their land resting from warfare (Ezek. 38:8) having signed a seven-year peace treaty with the Antichrist (Dan. 9:27). Just as the false prophets in   Jeremiah's day preached a false message of "peace, peace" right before their Babylonian oppressors arrived to decimate them (Jer. 4:10), the Jewish people will enjoy a short season of false peace just before suffering a terrible devastation in last half of the Tribulation Period.

The covenant will initially allow the Jews to dwell safely in unprotected villages in the land of Israel just prior to the battle of Gog and Magog (Ezek. 38:11). This phenomenon has not occurred in over 2,500 years and, at this present time, it is hard to imagine that the Jewish nation could ever be at peace with all their Arab neighbors and especially radical Islamist factions intent on annihilating them. Yet, the Antichrist will accomplish this seemingly incredible feat through promoting a one-world anti-God religion, which originated in Babylon. This religious reality is depicted as the harlot who rides the beast in Revelation 17.

The peace of the Antichrist is a temporary false peace which will engulf the world and allow him time to secure a political and economic system with himself at its head. Once in control, he will rid himself of the harlot, the religious system which served his worldwide agenda, and then claim to be God (Rev. 17:15-16). Anyone not pledging allegiance to him by taking his special mark, likely a technological means of economic transfer and global tracking, will be exterminated (Rev. 13:15-18; 20:4). Indeed, a great many will not bow to him and be slaughtered (Rev. 7:9-14).

The Battle of Gog and Magog

After centuries of oppression, the false peace of the Antichrist will be relished by the Jewish nation. But the peace treaty will be broken by the battle of Gog and Magog, which will likely occur just prior to the midpoint of the Tribulation Period. This battle should not be confused with the Battle of Gog and Magog at the end of Christ's millennial kingdom in which Satan gathers the nations to war, all of which are devoured by fire (Rev. 20:7-9). Jeremiah (Jer. 31), Ezekiel (Ezek. 38), and Joel (Joel 2) provide prophetic details of the future battle in the Tribulation Period. Ezekiel employs the Hebrew word *Rosh* to describe the land of Rosh, which will attack Israel during the battle of Gog and Magog:

Now the word of the Lord came to me, saying, "Son of man, set your face against Gog, of the land of Magog, the prince of Rosh, Meshech, and Tubal, and prophesy against him" (Ezek. 38:1-2).

And you, son of man, prophesy against Gog, and say, Thus says the Lord God: "Behold, I am against you, O Gog, the prince of Rosh, Meshech, and Tubal; and I will turn you around and lead you on, bringing you up from the far north, and bring you against the mountains of Israel" (Ezek. 39:1-3).

The land of Rosh lies directly north of Jerusalem (Ezek. 38:6, 15), and one must travel between two seas to arrive there (Joel 2:20). The Russian capital of "Moscow" may have its etymological roots in the ancient Hebrew word *Meshek* which is associated with Rosh in the above verses. It is noted that the ancient Greek derivation of this Hebrew word is *Moschoi*. Unlike many Russian cities, Moscow (*Moscva* in Russian) has not changed its name; it was called "Moscov" when founded in 1147.

What is known is that Magog, Meshek, and Tubal were all sons of Japheth (i.e., the grandsons of Noah) who settled in a region just south of present day Russia after the flood (Gen. 10:2). Accordingly, the people of Rosh, Magog, Meshek, and Tubal are all situated directly north of Jerusalem as one passes through Turkey and Georgia (which is between the Black and Caspian Seas). The prophets Joel and Ezekiel harmoniously describe the geographic location of the inhabitants of the region, home to those who invade Israel for a spoil during the Tribulation Period (Ezek. 38:12).

The Jews will be dwelling safely in unwalled villages when the attack comes from the north (Ezek. 38:8, 11, 14); they will be deceived into lowering their defenses while under the protection of the Antichrist's peace treaty (Dan. 9:27). Thankfully, the Lord will intervene and defeat not only the army of Rosh (Russia), but also the armies of Turkey, Germany, Iran, Ethiopia, and Egypt who ally with Rosh (Ezek. 38:5-6; Joel 2:12-20). While Jerusalem itself will be saved at that time, the persecution of the Jewish people worldwide will have only begun.

A Great Holocaust

In foretelling of the Antichrist and his endeavors during the Tribulation Period, the prophet Daniel provided a *predawn* prophecy of another evil man who would enter Israel under a banner of peace in order to slaughter the Jews (Dan. 8:9-14, 23-27). Daniel prophesied of Antiochus Epiphanes' assault on Israel nearly four centuries before it occurred. "Epiphanes" means "God made manifest" and Antiochus believed that he was the god Zeus.

In 168 BC, Antiochus led a second attack on Egypt, where he had been successful two years earlier. Before arriving at Alexandria, Gaius Popillius Laenas, a Roman ambassador, blocked his path to deliver a message from the Roman Senate warning Antiochus to withdraw his armies or consider himself at war with the Roman Republic. A humiliated Antiochus capitulated and withdrew his Seleucid army. Israel, a region he governed, was in the direct route home.

An enraged Antiochus entered Israel in 167 BC. After learning that his appointed high priest, Menelaus, had been deposed by a small group of Jews, including Jason whom Antiochus had earlier removed from that office, he sought vengeance on the Jewish people. Pretending to come in peace, a force of 22,000 soldiers entered Jerusalem.[3] They attacked the city on the Sabbath, knowing that orthodox Jews would not fight on their holy day (1 Mac. 1:31-35; 2 Mac. 5:24-26). As predicted by Daniel, the false pretenses of peace, the immense slaughter, the temple being desecrated, and the sacrifices being stopped all occurred (Dan. 11:31-32). The Abomination of Desolation that Daniel foretold then commenced: pigs were offered to Zeus on an altar erected on the Bronze Altar of burnt offerings (1 Mac. 1:54-61). As Antiochus considered himself to be Zeus, these sacrifices were in his honor. Many women and children were captured and made slaves. Jerusalem was plundered and burned. Judas Maccabees, a leader in the Jewish uprising, wrote of the heartbreaking incident:

> When these happenings were reported to the king, he thought that Judea was in revolt. Raging like a wild animal, he set out from Egypt and took Jerusalem by storm. He ordered his soldiers to cut down without mercy those whom they met and to slay those who took refuge in their houses. There was a massacre of young and old, a killing

of women and children, a slaughter of virgins and infants. In the space of three days, eighty thousand were lost, forty thousand meeting a violent death, and the same number being sold into slavery (2 Mac. 5:11-14).

Daniel also prophesied that a remnant of Jews would rise up against Antiochus and drive him from their beloved city (Dan. 11:32). It is likely that Antiochus departed and then returned to Jerusalem the following year to deal with the growing Jewish rebellion. Antiochus again departed from Jerusalem to deal with political unrest in Armenia and Persia. After hearing of yet another Jewish uprising, he sent Lysias to Jerusalem to exterminate the Jewish people; their land was to be confiscated and redistributed (1 Mac. 3:32-36). Lysias was soundly defeated by Judas Maccabeus and his freedom fighters on several occasions during the next year (1 Mac. 4:1-28) and finally withdrew from the region. After three years of intense fighting, the Jews won their liberation, recaptured Jerusalem, and regained control of the temple. On December 16, 164 BC, three years to the day after its desecration, the temple was cleansed and rededicated to Jehovah (1 Mac. 4:52-58). This Jewish triumph was still being celebrated annually in the days of Christ as the Feast of Dedication (John 10:22); however, it is more often identified today by its Hebrew name: *Hanukkah.*

Antiochus died of a sudden disease in 164 BC, shortly after he withdrew from Jerusalem. He is a type of the future Antichrist in that he desecrated the Jewish altar, stopped the Jewish sacrifices, sought to eradicate the Jewish people in a time of peace, and died shortly after doing so. Likewise, Daniel is forecasting that a time of peace and safety will briefly exist in Israel just before the Antichrist strikes the Jewish nation. In the last half of the Tribulation Period, he will seemingly convince the world that the Jews are the root of all the world's problems and must be eliminated. Thus, the immense carnage during the Babylonian invasion of Jeremiah's day serves as a precursor to more devastating events yet to come upon the Jewish people during the Tribulation Period.

When the abomination of desolation occurs at the midway point in the Tribulation Period, there will also be war in heaven. The archangel Michael, along with his angels, will war against the devil and his fallen angels in order to constrain evil to the earth (Dan. 12:1; Rev. 12:7-10). Satan, knowing that his time is short, will be enraged and seek to exterminate the Jewish people (Rev. 12:12-15). However, the Lord will preserve and protect a remnant of His covenant people from harm (Rev. 12:16-17).

During the Tribulation, there will be 144,000 Jews who are actively testifying of Jehovah (Rev. 7:4-8) and there will also be angels heralding the gospel message as they fly over the earth (Rev. 14:6-12). The devil knows that salvation is only possible while an individual is alive to choose Christ: *"And as it is appointed for men to die once, but after this the judgment"* (Heb. 9:27). Accordingly, he will attempt to exterminate all those who honor Jehovah or those who might hear and trust the kingdom gospel message. Satan will only spare those willing to take the mark of the beast and worship him. The Lord Jesus spoke of the horrific holocaust of life during this timeframe:

For then there will be great tribulation, such as has not been since the beginning of the world until this time, no, nor ever shall be. And unless those days were shortened, no flesh would be saved; but for the elect's sake those days will be shortened (Matt. 24:21-22).

If the Lord tarried longer than the appointed time to return to the earth, there would be no flesh left on the planet. Before the Tribulation Period concludes, the Antichrist will slaughter two-thirds of all Jews worldwide (Zech. 13:7-8). However, the Lord Jesus Christ will descend at the end of the Tribulation Period to protect and deliver His covenant people. As mentioned earlier, Jerusalem will be partially conquered when the Lord descends to engage the Antichrist at the battle of Armageddon (Zech. 14). This conflict will occur in the Megiddo Valley where the armies of the world will have assembled against the Jewish nation. The Lord will completely obliterate them all with just an utterance from His mouth (Rev. 19:11-20). Spiritual wickedness in high places and the masses of humanity under demonic delusion are no match for the Creator and Sustainer of all things.

National Spiritual Revival

With Christ's Second Advent to earth, the spiritual blindness of the Jewish nation will come to an end. They will trust in the Lord Jesus Christ, their Messiah, the One they had pierced two thousand years earlier (Zech. 12:10). In this spiritually fruitful state, the Jews will be known as the olive tree which provides a testimony of God's goodness to the entire world (Hos. 14:6; Rom. 11:17-24). Although we see that individual Jews in the Old Testament were filled by the Holy Spirit in order to speak for the Lord or to serve Him effectively (e.g., Ex. 35:30-35; 1 Sam. 10:10), the nation as a whole has never been indwelt by the Spirit of God (Zech. 4:4-7). This will not happen until Christ's second coming to the earth (Isa. 59:21).

This same truth is illustrated in Ezekiel's vision of the valley of dry bones. The Lord instructed Ezekiel to preach to a valley full of bones and, as he spoke, the bones began to move and assemble themselves into standing skeletons (Ezek. 37). This vision symbolizes the fact that the nation will be established again prior to its receiving spiritual life. After over 2,500 years of Gentile rule, Israel became its own political reality on May 14, 1948, even though the nation remains dead in a spiritual sense. The political birth of Israel coincides with the scriptural figure of the grape vine, not the olive tree. As Ezekiel continued to preach to the bones, the skeletons took on flesh. This great army now had the appearance of life, but in fact there was no life within them, corresponding to the image of the fig tree. Ezekiel then prophesied to the wind (a type of the Holy Spirit; John 3:8) to come and breathe life into the great standing army of dead men. This prophetic act signifies the spiritual birth of Israel and relates to their status as a productive olive tree.

During the Kingdom Age, which begins after Christ's Second Advent to the earth, the fig tree will bear fruit. Apparently, the Jews will be permitted by the Lord to again engage in some sacrifices and feasts at this time as a memorial of what God had accomplished for them through the ages (Ezek. 45; Zech. 14:16-21) in the same way that the Church today honors Christ by remembering Him and proclaiming the value of His death through the breaking of the bread (1 Cor. 11:24-30). Though the Lord's sacrifice of Himself occurred two thousand years ago, believers are not to forget what God accomplished for them in

Christ. It is noted that the *atoning* sacrifices offered by the Jews during the Kingdom Age (Ezek. 45:15-20) likely relate to ceremonial purification to ensure the millennial temple is not polluted by any unclean person (e.g., Lev. 8: 22-26; 14:4-7).

The Jewish millennial activities will occur in Jerusalem at the newly erected temple, the detailed dimensions and construction of which the prophet Ezekiel specified (Ezek. 40-43). Thus, the fig tree of the Old Testament, the visible religious system of the Jewish nation, will become fruitful in the millennial kingdom because it will have Christ as its true spiritual focus. Judaism, with all its extra-biblical traditions and interpretations, will have no part in the worship of the Jewish Messiah.

In the Kingdom Age, the Jews will have many reminders of the Mosaic system first practiced in the tabernacle, but these will not have the ritualistic significance as before, for a mere type cannot surpass its antitype, the real thing. Christ will be known as the fulfillment of all the Feasts of Jehovah, every article of priestly attire, each sacrifice and offering, and every aspect and furnishing of the tabernacle and temple. The spiritual realities conveyed through these Old Testament patterns will be understood and appreciated (Heb. 9:23). Christ's character and work will be vindicated and all His enemies will know that He is the eternal Son of God. He who has already been highly exalted and has a name above all others will be honored by all who remain on the earth!

A Coming Governor, Shepherd, and Plant of Renown

The prophet Jeremiah foretold of a day in which God would end Jewish captivity in Babylon and return the Jews to the Promised Land (Jer. 30:3-5). But then he spoke of another day afterwards in which God would again return His people to Israel from among all nations (Jer. 30:10-11). The Lord has scattered His covenant people throughout the nations to chasten them; indeed, they will be in a pitiful condition when He intervenes in the affairs of the world to bring them home once and for all (Jer. 30:12-13). Jeremiah thus implies that they would suffer centuries of God's chastisement for their unfaithfulness to Him and their love of false gods (Jer. 30:14-15).

Through Christ (their future Governor), God promised to restore them to the land to spiritually heal them, and also to punish those who have abused and despoiled them (Jer. 30:16-17): *"And their governor shall come from their midst; then I will cause him to draw near, and he shall approach Me"* (Jer. 30:21). Ezekiel speaks of a future day in which all Jews are back in Israel and each tribe will have their specific allotted territories (Ezek. 45). At that time, the nation shall be ruled by a Prince in righteousness. The Jewish nation shall readily bestow offerings to this Jewish Prince (Ezek. 45:16-17) and the Prince, acting as a priest, shall offer sacrifices on behalf of the nation (Ezek. 46:1-18). Whether the Prince is Christ Himself, or a vice-regent under His rule is debatable, but the fact remains this royal situation is yet future.

In the same chapter that Jeremiah introduces us to the coming Governor, he also speaks of the "Time of Jacob's Trouble." Jeremiah refers to this event as "that day," and said it would occur in "the latter days" (Jer. 30:24). As previously stated, this is a reference to the yet future Tribulation Period (Matt. 24:8-29). The Lord Jesus said that at no time before it, nor any time to come after it, will there be such suffering on the earth (Matt. 24:21). It is not a literal day, but a period of time in which Israel will suffer. Yet, ultimately, God will deliver them out of it. Ezekiel prophesied that God will seek His sheep through a great Shepherd that He will establish over His flock. This individual is also said to be "a Plant of Renown" (Ezek. 34:29) through whom tremendous blessing will be bestowed to the nation of Israel:

For thus says the Lord God: "Indeed I Myself will search for My sheep and seek them out. As a shepherd seeks out his flock on the day he is among his scattered sheep, so will I seek out My sheep and deliver them from all the places where they were scattered on a cloudy and dark day. And I will bring them out from the peoples and gather them from the countries, and will bring them to their own land; I will feed them on the mountains of Israel, in the valleys and in all the inhabited places of the country (Ezek. 34:11-13).

I will save My flock, and they shall no longer be a prey; and I will judge between sheep and sheep. I will establish one shepherd over them, and he shall feed them – My servant David. He shall feed them and be their shepherd. And I, the Lord, will be their God, and My servant David a prince among them; I, the Lord, have spoken (Ezek. 34:22-24).

"They shall be safe in their land; and they shall know that I am the Lord, when I have broken the bands of their yoke and delivered them from the hand of those who enslaved them. And they shall no longer be a prey for the nations, nor shall beasts of the land devour them; but they shall dwell safely, and no one shall make them afraid. I will raise up for them a garden of renown, and they shall no longer be consumed with hunger in the land, nor bear the shame of the Gentiles anymore. Thus they shall know that I, the Lord their God, am with them, and they, the house of Israel, are My people," says the Lord God. "You are My flock, the flock of My pasture; you are men, and I am your God," says the Lord God (Ezek. 34:27-31).

God moved the prophets to speak of various ministries of the coming Jewish Messiah. At His advent, He would gather His people from among the nations and then feed and protect them as a Shepherd. He would be a just and righteous Governor to rule over them, a Prince and Priest to make offerings to God on their behalf, and a Plant of Renown that would flourish in their presence and abundantly satisfy all their needs. Scripture carefully describes each of these Messianic blessings towards the Jewish people. A day is coming when the Lord Jesus Christ will watch over and care for His people forevermore.

The Sign of the Unknown Tongue

Old Testament Usage

Jeremiah repeatedly told the Jews that God would use the Babylonians as a rod of reproof against them for their continuing idolatry. One of the aspects of Jeremiah's preaching which especially infuriated the final four Judean kings was his message to submit to the Babylonians (Jer. 27). He warned that if they did not do so, Jerusalem would be destroyed and the nation would be exiled to Babylon (Jer. 22:5-10; 25:8-11). This demonstrates that God was willing to temper His discipline if His people humbly accepted His chastening. The Jews hated this message and, in time, plotted to kill God's messenger, Jeremiah (26:7-24).

But the people would not listen; they accused Jeremiah and the other godly prophets of being full of wind (Jer. 5:13). In response to this accusation, God declared that His words would instead be like a fire that would consume both the people and the land. **The people would know that judgment was near when they heard a language that they did not recognize** (Jer. 5:14-15). Eventually, Babylon destroyed Judah's best fortifications and battlements. Without the Lord's assistance to preserve them, the Jews had no hope of thwarting God's instrument of justice against them. What good is a high wall or a catapult against the God of the universe?

The sign of the unknown tongue is used throughout Scripture as a warning to the Jewish people of imminent judgment. Moses told the people that if they rebelled against the Lord, He would punish them through a nation whose language they would not understand (Deut. 28:49). This meant that God would use an army from a distant land instead of a neighboring nation. Isaiah warned idolatrous Israel by imposing this sign just prior to the Assyrian invasion (Isa. 28:11-12) and Jeremiah referenced it as a final warning to Judah of imminent judgment for the same deeply-rooted sin (Jer. 5:15). But the Jews ignored the warnings of Moses, Isaiah, and Jeremiah; the sign of the unknown tongue was issued and severe judgment ultimately came. Yet, this was not the last time God would use the sign of an unknown tongue to alert the Jews of impending judgment for their unfaithfulness.

New Testament Usage

According to Acts 2:9-11, ten specific languages were heard in Jerusalem at the Feast of Pentecost, just after Christ's ascension into heaven. This was the day the Church Age began (Acts 2:4; 1 Cor. 12:13). The Holy Spirit came to the believers as promised by the Lord Jesus, baptized them into the body of Christ, bestowed spiritual gifts on them, and enabled them to supernaturally serve the Lord. This event served two main purposes. First, it verified in the sight of the Jews that the apostles were continuing the ministry of Christ and were doing so by His power (Acts 2:22). Second, it served as a final warning to the nation of Israel to repent and turn to God through Christ. As a nation, they had rejected and crucified their Messiah, but, as individuals, they now had the opportunity to be saved. Unavoidable judgment was coming upon the nation of Israel and trusting Christ for salvation was the only way for them to obtain God's forgiveness.

In AD 70, that crushing judgment came. A vast Roman army of about 70,000 soldiers was led by the future Emperor Titus to besiege and conquer Jerusalem. The temple that had been built by the Jewish captives who returned from Babylon towards the end of the sixth century BC and that had then been renovated by Herod the Great some five centuries later was destroyed. There were to be no more offerings, sacrifices, Levitical priesthood, or stench of humanized religion in the nostrils of Jehovah. Even to this day, although the Jews are back in their land and are a self-governing nation, they have no temple or priesthood to reinstate what God put away. Why? The writer of Hebrews explains:

For if that first covenant had been faultless, then no place would have been sought for a second. Because finding fault with them, He says: "Behold, the days are coming, says the Lord, when I will make a new covenant with the house of Israel and with the house of Judah – not according to the covenant that I made with their fathers in the day when I took them by the hand to lead them out of the land of Egypt; because they did not continue in My covenant, and I disregarded them, says the Lord. For this is the covenant that I will make with the house of Israel after those days, says the Lord: I will put My laws in their mind and write them on their hearts; and I will be their God, and they shall be My people.... In that He says, "A new covenant," He has made the first obsolete. Now what is becoming obsolete and growing old is ready to vanish away (Heb. 8:7-13).

About three to five years after these words were penned, God used the Romans to completely remove the religious practices of the Old Covenant from Israel. In reality, these had already been replaced by the New Covenant, which had been sealed with Christ's blood forty years earlier. But the Jews had rejected the terms of this covenant which required them to receive Christ as their Messiah. Through the destruction of Jerusalem and the temple, God put an end to the Levitical order established by the Old Covenant, a system that the Jews had humanized into their own religion (Gal. 1:13-14). No more ceremonial lip service would be offered to God. Given what Jehovah had already secured by the judgment of His own Son, such religious hype was offensive to Him.

Through the New Covenant, and through it alone, God would forgive the sins of Israel and Judah, pour out His Spirit upon them, and restore them to Himself. Some Christians, like Paul, were bestowed the sign gift of speaking in a foreign tongue to warn Israel to trust Christ and thus avoid imminent judgment (1 Cor. 14:18). This is why Paul did not forbid others who also had this sign gift from speaking in a foreign language in the Church, if there was an interpreter (1 Cor. 14:39). The unknown tongue was a sign to the lost (1 Cor. 14:22), especially to his Jewish countrymen, whom Paul greatly desire to be saved (Rom. 9:3; 10:1).

This supernatural gift apparently diminished in normalcy during the Apostolic Age, as there is no mention of it in Scripture after AD 60. It is significant that over half the New Testament was written after this timeframe. Although the New Testament does record the names of many Jews who did turn from Judaism to Christ, Israel, as a nation, rejected Him and will continue to do so until His second advent at the end of the Tribulation Period (Joel 2:18-3:21; Isa. 11:1-16; Ezek. 36:16-38; Zech. 12:10).

Future Usage

The prophet Joel informs us that the Lord will one last time allow Israel to be surrounded by many nations (i.e., many tongues) and be threatened with utter destruction. This will happen just prior to Christ's return to Jerusalem to protect and restore Israel. As mentioned earlier, Zechariah 14 states that Jerusalem will have fallen at this time, but the Lord will deliver His people and judge the nations for harming the apple of His eye. In this way, God is working with His covenant people and invoking justice on the wicked at the same time; He has done this consistently throughout Jewish history. Joel writes:

For behold, in those days and at that time, when I bring back the captives of Judah and Jerusalem, I will also gather all nations, and bring them down to the Valley of Jehoshaphat; and I will enter into judgment with them there on account of My people, My heritage Israel, whom they have scattered among the nations; they have also divided up My land (Joel 3:1-2).

Proclaim this among the nations: "Prepare for war! Wake up the mighty men, let all the men of war draw near, let them come up" (Joel 3:9).

"Let the nations be wakened, and come up to the Valley of Jehoshaphat; for there I will sit to judge all the surrounding nations" (Joel 3:12).

Multitudes, multitudes in the valley of decision! For the day of the Lord is near in the valley of decision. The sun and moon will grow dark, and the stars will diminish their brightness. The Lord also will roar from Zion, and utter His voice from Jerusalem; the heavens and earth will shake; but the Lord will be a shelter for His people, and the strength of the children of Israel. "So you shall know that I am the Lord your God dwelling in Zion My holy mountain. Then Jerusalem shall be holy, and no aliens shall ever pass through her again" (Joel 3:14-17).

The presence of so many foreign tongues will again signal to the Jewish nation that imminent judgment is forthcoming and that they must repent and turn to the only one who can save them – the Lord Jesus Christ. The prophet Joel also acknowledges that the remnant of the nation, those who have not been slaughtered by the Antichrist, will trust Christ and receive the Holy Spirit.

Then you shall know that I am in the midst of Israel: I am the Lord your God and there is no other. My people shall never be put to shame. And it shall come to pass afterward that I will pour out My Spirit on all flesh; ... the sun shall be turned into darkness, and the moon into blood, before the coming of the great and awesome day of the Lord. And it shall come to pass that whoever calls on the name of the Lord shall be saved. For in Mount Zion and in Jerusalem there shall be deliverance, as the Lord has said, among the remnant whom the Lord calls (Joel 2:27-32).

Peter quoted this portion of Scripture on the day of Pentecost to acknowledge that Joel's prophecy had been partially fulfilled (i.e., when Jewish believers were suddenly able to speak in various other languages). It is therefore possible that the 144,000 sealed Jewish witnesses of Revelation 7 may be equipped with the supernatural gift of tongues again. This would both signal Israel of the coming judgment and provide the means for Jews to convey the gospel to all people groups in their own language.

Summary

According to Genesis 11, paganism finds its roots in Nimrod at Babel. It is noted that our English word *Babylon* is simply the word *Babel* with a Greek ending. Nimrod caused the people of the earth to congregate in one location against God's command and then to erect a tower up to heaven so they could be like God. Jehovah confused man's languages because of their rebellion, but three millennia later, He gave the ability of speaking different languages to obedient Jewish believers who were waiting in Jerusalem, as instructed by Christ, for the coming of the Holy Spirit.

On the Feast of Pentecost, the awaiting Jewish believers were baptized into Christ to form His body the Church and were filled and gifted to declare the good news of Christ in various distinct languages (Acts 2:4-11). Peter confirmed that the event was a partial fulfillment of Joel's prophecy. The foreigners visiting Jerusalem for the feast were able to hear the gospel message in their own tongue. Just as the hearing of foreign tongues in the Old Testament served as a warning to the Jews that divine judgment was near, so, too, the same warning sign was given at Pentecost. Based on Joel 2, this will likely be the case in the Tribulation Period also.

In Genesis, the confusion of languages, and in Acts, the understanding of languages, both resulted in the message of God's greatness to be carried over all the earth! This blessing will also occur during the Tribulation Period. Accordingly, a testimony of God's abundant grace was foreseen by John; people speaking *every* known tongue will be about the heavenly throne praising God forever and ever (Rev. 7:9). There will be no unknown tongues in God's presence!

Babylon Destroyed Forever

The destruction of Jerusalem by the Babylonians in 586 BC marked the beginning of a new era called *"the times of the Gentiles"* (Luke 21:24). This period of time continues even now, for although the Jews gained independence in May 1948 after 2,600 years of Gentile rule, they are still in a constant state of war with Gentiles. Daniel said that this would be the case until the Tribulation Period when, at the battle of Armageddon, the times of the Gentiles will end (Dan. 9:27; Luke 21:24; Rev. 11:2). The Lamb shall return from heaven to be the Victor and establish His covenant people in His presence forever. The times of the Gentiles began when Babylon conquered Jerusalem and will conclude when Christ destroys Babylon once and for all at His Second Advent.

John refers to the religious and economic system established by the Antichrist to rule the world as "Babylon" several times in Revelation chapters 17 and 18. Babylon represents the religious world system that began under Nimrod and will have its final destruction during the Tribulation Period, just prior to the establishment of Christ's kingdom on earth. As in the days of Zedekiah, which started the times of the Gentiles, the nations, led by the Antichrist, will again attempt to conquer Jerusalem and slaughter the Jews. The prophet Zechariah informs us that many Jews will die in this attack and that Jerusalem will be captured before the Lord Jesus returns to defeat the invaders and put an end to Antichrist and his worldwide system of control. The fall of Babylon will conclude the times of the Gentiles.

From the book of Revelation, we learn that the Antichrist's political and economic system is identified with Babylon and will be destroyed by Christ at His second advent (Rev. 18). The religious aspect of this system, which the Antichrist will use to gain control of the world, will actually be eliminated by the Antichrist himself during the middle portion of the Tribulation Period (Rev. 17). This event coincides with what is called "the Abomination of Desolation." At that time, the Antichrist will no longer tolerate the one-world religion he helped create; he will demand to be worshipped as god himself (2 Thess. 2:4-7). The Antichrist will destroy the last religious system of humanism, which began with Nimrod in Babylon of old: *"MYSTERY, BABYLON THE GREAT, THE MOTHER OF HARLOTS AND OF THE ABOMINATIONS OF THE EARTH"* (Rev. 17:5). This religious system is responsible for the death of millions of God's people throughout the course of human history. The harlot, as John describes her, is *"drunk with the blood of the saints"* (Rev. 17:6).

With this understanding, we now turn our attention to specific prophesies pertaining to the future destruction of Babylon recorded in Jeremiah 50. The prophet begins by proclaiming that Babylon will be attacked and conquered by an army from the north and that Babylon's chief deity, Bel, also known as Marduk, will not be able to avert this calamity. The city of Babylon itself will be laid waste (i.e., destroyed by fire – Jer. 50:32) and uninhabited, and the nation as a whole will be put to shame (Jer. 50:13). The Babylonians will be filled with terror and suffer the same fate that they had inflicted on so many others. God had used Babylon as an instrument of chastening, but they were a pagan nation also deserving of judgment for their own wickedness and atrocities against their fellow man.

Have these prophecies already been fulfilled or do they have a future application? History records that the Medes and the Persians, under the command of Cyrus, conquered the city of Babylon in 539 BC. However, extra-biblical documentation of this conquest does not confirm the descriptions Jeremiah and Isaiah provide of Babylon's destruction or their prophecy that the city would be uninhabitable (Isa. 13:17-22; Jer. 50-51). Reviewing what we know of ancient Babylon, how it fell to the Persians, and what became of the city afterwards, will be helpful in substantiating this conclusion.

The Greek historian Herodotus, writing in the fifth century BC, recorded the following information about ancient Babylon at the time of its conquest:[1]

- The city was in the form of a square (each side was fourteen miles in length).

- The outer brick wall surrounding the city was 56 miles long, 300 feet high, 25 feet thick, and had a base that extended 35 feet below the ground.
- An inner wall of 75 feet in height was behind the first wall.
- The city had 250 towers that were each 450 feet high.
- The Euphrates River flowed through and around the city which provided it with a deep and wide moat for protection.
- Access to the city was gained either through ferry boats or a half-mile-long bridge which had drawbridges that were closed at night.
- The city had eight massive gates and 100 brass gates leading to the inner city.
- The streets of Babylon were paved with stone slabs 3 feet square.
- Within the city was a great tower (a ziggurat) and fifty-three temples, including the Great Temple of Marduk.

The famous walls of Babylon were indeed impenetrable. The only way into the city was through its gates or by the Euphrates River, which flowed through submersed passages in and out of the city. On this last point, the Babylonians had built metal grids at each point where the river flowed in and out of the city to prevent underwater intrusions. However, while Babylon was under siege, Cyrus' corps of engineers devised a way of diverting the Euphrates River away from Babylon. Persian troops were placed at strategic points around the city, waiting until the water level dropped. The plan was executed on the evening of a Babylonian feast (Dan. 5). At the appropriate time, Cyrus' engineers diverted the Euphrates river upstream, which caused it to drop to or below "mid-thigh level on a man," according to Herodotus. With the water level brought down, Cyrus' soldiers were able to enter the city by marching under the gated walls. The Persian army swiftly conquered the outer city while most of the Babylonians were still feasting in the city center, oblivious to the breach and invasion force.[2]

At the time Babylon fell, Nabunaid (Nabonidus) shared its kingship with his oldest son Belshazzar. The Nabonidus Chronicle provides the exact date in which Cyrus conquered Babylon:

In the month of Tashritu on the fourteenth day, October 10, 539 BC, the Persian forces took Sippar; on the sixteenth day, October 12, "the army of Cyrus entered Babylon without battle;" and in the month of Arahsamnu, on the third day, October 29, Cyrus himself came into the city.[3]

Thus, Babylon fell to the Persians on October 12, 539 BC.

Two hundred years prior to these events, the prophet Isaiah foretold by name the man whom God would use to defeat the Babylonians: Cyrus. He would punish the Babylonians, end the Jewish exile, and initiate the rebuilding of the temple in Jerusalem (Isa. 44:28-45:4). But did Cyrus destroy the city of Babylon by fire? Was it uninhabited afterwards, as Jeremiah prophesied? The answer to these questions is, "No." Cyrus used Babylon as a Persian outpost, but through the centuries, Babylon gradually lost its political influence throughout the Persian Empire. The population of Babylon declined over the next two hundred years and, ultimately, the city was dismantled under the Greek Empire to provide building materials for other cities. In short, Jeremiah's prophecies concerning the method of Babylon's destruction have yet to be fulfilled.

When one compares the historical evidence and the specific declarations of Isaiah and Jeremiah, it becomes evident that many of their prophecies pertaining to the fall of Babylon remain unfulfilled:

- Babylon's walls and foundations were not suddenly thrown down into heaps (Jer. 50:15, 22, 26; 51:8, 44).
- Babylon was not destroyed by fire, like Sodom and Gomorrah (Jer. 51:25, 30, 32, 40; Isa. 13:19).
- Babylon was not conquered by a northern army (Jer. 50:3, 9, 41; 51:48) – the Persians came from the east.
- Babylon was not conquered by an army composed of a conglomeration of many nations (Jer. 50:9, 41, 46).
- Babylon was not made uninhabitable after it was conquered (Jer. 50:3, 45; 51:37; Isa. 12:20-21).
- The inhabitants of Babylon, including the Jews, did not flee from the city before its capture by the Medo-Persian army (Jer. 50:8; 51:5-6); in fact, we know from Scripture that Daniel and other Jews remained in the city (Dan. 5:28-6:3).
- Through the destruction of Babylon, some of the Jews were brought back to their homeland (Jer. 50:4-5, 19), but did not enter

into *"a perpetual covenant"* with God that would never be forgotten (Jer. 50:5).

- Although the sword of the Lord was certainly against Babylon through the hand of Cyrus (Jer. 51:11), the promised Great Redeemer who would bring peace to Israel has not yet come (Jer. 50:34-37).

We conclude that the events related to Babylon's capture in the sixth century BC and its eventual demise centuries later do not conform to the specific prophecies of Isaiah and Jeremiah. To date, for example, Babylon has never been destroyed by fire. Since the Lord says that it must be destroyed by fire, the rebuilding of a city known as Babylon is guaranteed (Rev. 18:10). Another prophecy regarding Babylon further substantiates this point: *"They shall not take from you a stone for a corner nor a stone for a foundation, but you shall be desolate forever."* (Jer. 51:26). Reliable evidence shows that at least six cities contain building materials which originally belonged to ancient Babylon. Hillah, which is near ancient Babylon, was built almost entirely from its ruins. Over two hundred years after the city's fall to Cyrus, one of Alexander the Great's successors, Seleucus, nearly demolished ancient Babylon to obtain resources to build a new city some 30 miles away.[4] According to the Bible, when Babylon is destroyed by fire, it will never be inhabited again, nor will debris from its ruins be profitable for reuse. Since this type of destruction has yet to occur, when might the fulfillment of this prophecy come to pass?

Two clues are found in Jeremiah 50:19-20. That prophecy declares that Israel will regain Bashan as a possession and no iniquity will be found in either Judah or Israel. As previously acknowledged, Bashan (the Golan Heights in northeastern Israel) did not become a Jewish possession until after the Six Day War of 1967. Thus, the fulfillment of the destruction of Babylon could not have occurred before this. Moreover, we know that the Jews will walk with the Lord in a state of righteousness only after they have been brought into the good of the perpetual covenant (50:5) by trusting Jesus Christ as their Savior and receiving the Holy Spirit. This will be a national event occurring at the end of the Tribulation Period (Ezek. 36:24-27). These clues, then, point to a yet future fulfillment of Jeremiah's prophecy concerning the judgment of Babylon.

A third clue is found in Revelation 18. John informs us that Babylon will be destroyed suddenly (Rev. 18:8, 10, 17, 19), by fire (Rev. 18:8-9, 18), suffer complete destruction (Rev. 18:21), and remain uninhabited forever (Rev. 18:22). Indeed, John reconfirms much of what Jeremiah and Isaiah predicted concerning Babylon's final destruction seven hundred years earlier. Whether the Babylon spoken of in Revelation 18 refers to an entire kingdom or a specific city is unknown, but it is noted that Saddam Hussein began rebuilding the city of Babylon upon its ancient foundations in 1983. However, after the Iraq War and the deposition of Hussein from power, much of the construction work ceased and the site has become merely a tourist attraction. The city was never fully established; perhaps it will be before all that is connected with Babylon is wiped out during the Tribulation Period.

Returning to the events in Jeremiah's day, why did God promise to punish Babylon? Two main reasons are given in the book of Jeremiah. First, God vowed, *"I will bring judgment on the carved images of Babylon"* (Jer. 51:47). God hates paganism; it robs Him of His rightful honor as Almighty God, Lord Supreme, and Creator of All. Second, He promised, *"I will repay Babylon and all the inhabitants of Chaldea for all the evil they have done in Zion in your sight"* (Jer. 51:24). We learned in an earlier chapter that the Jews are the apple of God's eye, His covenant people. Zechariah proclaimed that any nation that persecutes the Jews will ultimately be judged by God: *"For thus says the Lord of hosts, 'He sent Me after glory, to the nations which plunder you; for he who touches you touches the apple of His eye'"* (Zech. 2:8). Babylon is no exception.

Looking into the future, why will the Lord Jesus Christ destroy wicked Babylon at His second coming? Because the anti-God spirit that started in Nimrod's time will ultimately culminate in Babylon with the political and religious system of the Antichrist in the Tribulation Period. As previously mentioned, this rebel movement has been responsible for the deaths of millions of God's people: *"In her [Babylon] was found the blood of prophets and saints, and of all who were slain on the earth"* (Rev. 18:24). Also, God will judge all those who have oppressed and persecuted His people down through the ages. In Jeremiah's day, the fall of Babylon signaled that the time of Jewish chastening had ended and that it was time for the Jews to return to Israel to enjoy

God's protection and blessing there. The future fall of Babylon will indicate the same things, only ever so much more.

The exiled Jews in Babylon would have understood Jeremiah's prophecies concerning the fall of Babylon and their return to Zion to pertain to them personally. But we have the advantage of more scriptural revelation concerning the future of Babylon and we also have the benefit of history to more fully understand what Jeremiah was writing about – the final destruction of Babylon during the Tribulation Period.

Certainly the soon-coming restoration of the Jews to their homeland after Cyrus captured Babylon was in the mind of God, for Jeremiah had before proclaimed that truth many times. However, the spiritual unification of the Lord Jesus Christ with His covenant people after He destroys all that Babylon stands for is what thrills the heart of God and is the chief view of this passage of Scripture. The Lord greatly desires to be with His covenant people and for His people to walk with Him!

The Exodus Connection

As already stated, the Tribulation Period will be a seven-year period of immense suffering for the Jewish nation. Jeremiah refers to this period as "the time of Jacob's trouble," which is first introduced to us as a *type* in Genesis. During the days of Joseph, a devastating seven-year famine affected the whole land; this pictures the future seven-year Tribulation Period that will ravage the entire planet. When used metaphorically, *Egypt* speaks of the world in Scripture. Just as the nation of Israel was protected and preserved by God in Egypt during this severe seven-year trial, it will also be protected from the Antichrist during the Tribulation Period (Rev. 12).

A Pattern of the Tribulation Period

Beside symbolic representation of the Tribulation Period in Genesis, the following book, Exodus, foreshadows many of the future events recorded in the book of Revelation. The plagues brought upon Egypt in the days of Moses are undeniably similar to those unleashed upon the entire world during the Tribulation Period, especially that last three and a half years called the Great Tribulation. For example, the fifth trump judgment will release from the bottomless pit armored locusts which sting like scorpions (Rev. 9:1-12); recall that locusts ravaged Egypt in the eighth plague (Ex. 10:1-20). The second and third bowl judgments towards the end of the Tribulation Period turn all the ocean water and all the fresh water, respectively, into blood (Rev. 16:3-7). This reminds us of the events of Exodus 7:14-25, when Moses turned the Nile into blood, which killed all life in the river. The fifth bowl judgment causes darkness throughout the Antichrist's kingdom (Rev. 16:10-11); Moses' ninth plague caused three days of intense darkness in Egypt (Ex. 10:21-29).

Though the plagues and the seven-year famine brought devastation to Egypt, God preserved the Jewish nation through the hardship and then greatly blessed them afterwards. This typological illustration has its fulfillment in the Tribulation Period. God will protect His covenant people from the attempts of the Antichrist to exterminate them and He will pour His blessings upon them afterwards in the millennial kingdom.

In Moses' day, God poured out His wrath upon the Egyptians because they abused the Hebrews and defied Him. God's judgment on Egypt is only a prelude to what the entire world will suffer during the Tribulation Period for the same two reasons. The Egyptian plagues furnished a striking prophetic forecast of God's future judgments upon the world! During the Tribulation Period, the wrath of the Lamb will be worldwide, not merely restricted to a single nation, such as Egypt.

The actions of Pharaoh's sorcerers picture future supernatural feats to be accomplished by the Antichrist and False Prophet during the Tribulation Period. These will also be performed through demonic power (Rev. 16:14). The interactions between the magicians and Moses demonstrated not only Jehovah's superior authority and power, but also the fact that Jehovah would judge the Egyptian gods and all who worshipped them. The same truth will be demonstrated during the Tribulation Period against all who follow the Antichrist and receive his mark (Rev. 14:9-11; 19:20-21).

The Song of the Redeemed

Another significant parallel between the events recorded in Exodus and those recorded in Revelation is the singing. The last mention of singing in the Bible is associated with the first song recorded in the Bible – it is the song of the redeemed Israelites after seeing their oppressors were vanquished in the Red Sea (Ex. 15). In the book of Revelation, John describes the following heavenly scene:

And I saw something like a sea of glass mingled with fire, and those who have the victory over the beast, over his image and over his mark and over the number of his name, standing on the sea of glass, having harps of God. They sing the song of Moses, the servant of God, and the song of the Lamb, saying:

Great and marvelous are Your works,
Lord God Almighty! Just and true are Your ways,

O King of the saints!
Who shall not fear You, O Lord, and glorify Your name?
For You alone are holy.
For all nations shall come and worship before You,
For Your judgments have been manifested (Rev. 15:2-4).

This song will be sung again, not by those just escaping death to journey with Jehovah through the wilderness, but rather by those who will journey to Him in heaven through death to escape the Antichrist. These saints will choose death rather than to bow to the Antichrist. The heavenly inheritance sung of by the Israelites long ago will then be theirs to enjoy forever. Furthermore, God's own joy in His redeemed people is enthusiastically expressed in song directly after the Tribulation when He will sing over His people (Zeph. 3:17).

The twelve Tribes of Israel were numbered when they departed Egypt under Moses' leadership. Similarly, during the first part of the Tribulation Period, there will be 144,000 Jews (12,000 Jews from each tribe) who are counted and sealed to be witnesses for the Lord: *"And I heard the number of those who were sealed, one hundred and forty-four thousand of all the tribes of the children of Israel were sealed"* (Rev. 7:4). After these faithful Jews have completed their ministry in the Tribulation Period, we read:

Then I looked, and behold, a Lamb standing on Mount Zion, and with Him one hundred and forty-four thousand, having His Father's name written on their foreheads.... They sang as it were a new song before the throne, before the four living creatures, and the elders; and no one could learn that song except the hundred and forty-four thousand who were redeemed from the earth. These are the ones who were not defiled with women, for they are virgins. These are the ones who follow the Lamb wherever He goes. These were redeemed from among men, being firstfruits to God and to the Lamb. And in their mouth was found no deceit, for they are without fault before the throne of God (Rev. 14:1-5).

What the Jews first sang in Exodus after being redeemed and delivered from their oppressors in Egypt will be the song they sing before the Lord after being saved from the Antichrist.

Summary

Many of the Old Testament narratives which detail God's dealings for His covenant people also provide a prophetic blueprint for how He will accomplish their final spiritual conversion. It took the Babylonian exile and the destruction of the temple and Jerusalem to purge the Jews of idolatry in Jeremiah's day. Likewise, during the Time of Jacob's Trouble, God will use immense suffering to open the eyes of the Jewish nation to the unsearchable riches of the Lord Jesus Christ. Through the Refiner's fire (Mal. 3:3-4), they will no longer be reprobate silver (Jer. 6:30), but will become purified silver which reflects the Refiner's own features. The Jewish people will be established with God and blessed by Him forever!

Jeremiah's "Beholds"

The Old Covenant could never make Israel a well-watered garden because they could not keep it (Jer. 31:12); a New Covenant was necessary – one that would result in the supernatural transformation of the nation. Jeremiah introduced this subject in one of his messages by employing three statements beginning with the word "behold"; each speaks of a separate future event (Jer. 31:27-40):

The First Behold – Jews and Agricultural Blessings Restored

The first occurrence is found in Jeremiah 31:27: *"Behold, the days are coming, says the Lord, that I will sow the house of Israel and the house of Judah with the seed of man and the seed of beast."* Here the Jews were promised that, in a coming day, after the captivity, God would again sow the seeds of men and beast in the Promised Land. The land would be decimated by the Babylonians and made unusable, but God would restore His covenant people to the land in order to bless them and to care for them in that place (Jer. 31:28).

Jeremiah foretold that some Jews exiled in Babylon would feel that they had been wrongly judged by God for the sins of their forefathers and would banter about the proverb, *"The fathers have eaten sour grapes, and the children's teeth are set on edge"* (Jer. 31:29). In short, the proverb insinuated that the exiles were suffering for their parents' sins, not their own. However, this would not be the case; everyone will be rightly judged by God for his own sins (Jer. 31:30). For decades, Jeremiah and other prophets had called upon the Jews to consider their sin and its consequences and to repent. The Jews taken into captivity had earned that judgment: they were not innocent and had indeed received mercy from God in that they were still alive.

The Second Behold – A New Covenant Is Necessary

The second injunction to behold relates to the Lord's promise to institute a New Covenant with the houses of Judah and Israel (Jer. 31:31-32):

Behold, the days are coming, says the Lord, when I will make a new covenant with the house of Israel and with the house of Judah – not according to the covenant that I made with their fathers in the day that I took them by the hand to lead them out of the land of Egypt, My covenant which they broke, though I was a husband to them, says the Lord.

Jeremiah says that this would be an everlasting covenant resulting in eternal blessing to the Jews (32:40). This promise is understood to be literal, for God will erect an eternal city where the Jewish remnant will dwell (Isa. 48:2; 52:1). The prophet Ezekiel refers to the New Covenant as a *"Covenant of Peace"* with the Jewish nation (Ezek. 34:25). Isaiah proclaimed that through this covenant, *"Israel shall be saved in the Lord with an everlasting salvation"* (Isa. 45:17).

Why was the New Covenant needed and how did it secure such blessing for Israel? The writer of Hebrews informs us that this covenant was sealed by Christ's blood and would accomplish what the Old Covenant could not – propitiation for sins (Heb. 8:8). The Old Covenant was conditional in nature; the Jews had to keep God's Law to receive God's blessing (Ex. 19:5-8; Heb. 8:9). The New Covenant would be unconditional in nature and would be the means by which God would honor His covenant with Abraham, which was instituted by two immutable things – God's word and His oath (Heb. 6:13-18), neither of which can fail.

One may then wonder how the Gentiles could be brought into the goodness of the New Covenant, if it was strictly instituted between Jehovah and Israel. William Kelly addresses this question:

I do not say we, Christians, have got the new covenant itself, but we have got the blood of the new covenant. We have that on which the new covenant is founded. The new covenant itself supposes the land of Israel blessed and the house of Israel delivered, but neither the one nor the other has become true yet. The new covenant supposes certain spiritual blessings, namely, the law of God written in the heart and our sins forgiven. These spiritual parts of the new covenant we have received now, along with other blessings peculiar to Christianity, namely, the presence of the Holy Ghost and union with Christ in heaven which the Jews will not have. But nothing can be more evident than that this prophecy refutes the Jew when he imagines that it is a dishonor to the law for God to bring in anything better than what was enjoyed in the days of Moses.[1]

God, in His mercy, permitted the Gentiles to come into the blessing of the New Covenant as a second benefactor of His promise to bless Abraham's descendants (Eph. 2:14-3:8). Gentiles can only enter into the blessing of this covenant by following Abraham's example of trusting God's word by faith; in this way, they become spiritual descendants of Abraham and are able to partake of the spiritual blessings promised to his descendants (Rom. 4:11-17).

Through the New Covenant, God is able to righteously justify sinners if they trust Christ alone for salvation (Rom. 4:23-25). Those who do so receive the gift of the Holy Spirit (John 14:16-17; 1 Cor. 12:12-13). Thus, through the gospel of Jesus Christ, those who were not God's people (the Gentiles) can become His children (Rom. 9:25-26). It is only by the power of the Holy Spirit that believers are able to both understand the law of God and to fulfill its righteousness (1 Cor. 2:11-15; Rom. 8:4-17).

Likewise, once Israel is fully restored to God at the end of the Tribulation Period, the Holy Spirit will ensure that they will never leave Him again for false gods; instead, they will continue in His Law. As a nation, they will receive the Holy Spirit, and He will give them a new heart (Joel 2:27-29; Ezek. 36:23-28). As a result, God's Law will be deep inside them (Jer. 31:33). In that day, all the Jews from the oldest to the youngest will intimately know Jehovah and identify Him as *"The Lord of Hosts"* (Jer. 31: 34-35). God cannot lie and His word is eternal, and so shall His blessing be towards His people (Jer. 31: 36-37).

The Third Behold – Christ's Future Kingdom

The third and final "behold" statement relates to the Millennial Kingdom (Jer. 31:38): *"Behold, the days are coming, says the Lord, that the city shall be built for the Lord from the Tower of Hananel to the Corner Gate."* Jerusalem will be a city built for the Lord, it will be the religious center of the world, and the entire land of Israel will be holy to the Lord (Jer. 31:39-40; Isa. 66:10-21; Zech. 14:17).

The Millennial Kingdom of Christ will begin directly after *The Judgment of Nations* at the conclusion of the Tribulation Period. The Lord Jesus taught about this judgment in the seventh of the Kingdom Parables found in Matthew 13:47-50. In that parable, the Lord casts a net into the sea (depicting the nations – Rev. 17:1, 15) and sorts through that which is caught. Those who did not follow the Antichrist are separated from those who did. The "good" are permitted into His kingdom; the "bad" are committed to eternal judgment. The net represents the influence of the kingdom gospel message that will be preached worldwide during the Tribulation Period (Matt. 24:14). This message consists of a warning not to worship the Antichrist and a declaration that judgment of the wicked and Christ's kingdom are coming soon (Rev. 14:6-12). The fish represent the living Gentiles who are saved during the Tribulation Period. The Judgment of Nations is more specifically spoken of in Matthew 25:31-46 when the Lord separates the sheep (i.e., those who are allowed into the kingdom) and the goats (those who eternally judged). Christ will punish all those who followed the Antichrist and persecuted the Jews during the Tribulation Period (Matt. 25:40). This judgment will occur just after Christ's return to the earth at the end of the Great Tribulation (Matt. 24:21, 29, 36-41) and will not be expected by the general populous. The Judgment of Nations is done suddenly and those unfit for the kingdom will be abruptly removed from the earth. The Judgment of Nations is also pictured in Daniel 2:35, 44-45 and described in Revelation 19:20.

Daniel informs us that there will be a 75-day interval between the destruction of the Antichrist at the battle of Armageddon and the beginning of the blessings of the Kingdom Age (Dan. 12:7-13; Rev. 17-21). This time period is necessary to cleanse the earth of defilement and the devastation which occurred in the previous seven years. Daniel illustrates this truth through his interpretation of Nebuchadnezzar's dream in which the stone from heaven (Christ) falls to the earth and smashes an image representing all Gentile dominion throughout the ages. The debris is then blown away by the wind and, afterwards, the stone grows into a great mountain. The Spirit of God is pictured in the wind (John 3:8) and mountains in Scripture are used to symbolize kingdoms (Isa. 2:2-3; Mic. 4:1; Rev. 17:9-10). But after all wickedness has been purged from the planet and it has been supernaturally rejuvenated to nullify the effects of sin, Jerusalem will be the seat of God's glory on the earth.

The Lord's Second Advent to the earth will conclude the period of time that the Gentiles were allowed to rule over Israel (Rom. 11:25). This event also coincides with the end of Israel's spiritual blindness (Rom. 11:7-14). When Christ ventured to the earth two thousand years ago, He removed the veil God had put over the Law (i.e., its full purpose was not disclosed until after Christ's ascension to heaven), but the Jews picked the veil back up and blindfolded themselves to the truth (2 Cor. 3:6-18). The purpose of the Mosaic Law was to show the Jews their sin (Rom. 3:20) and to point them to the solution: Christ (Gal. 3:24). At Calvary, Christ satisfied all of the judicial claims of the Law by substitutionally dying in the place of sinners. By rejecting His kingdom gospel message, the Jews became locked into a state of blindness, a condition that Satan works hard to maintain (2 Cor. 4:4).

However, during the Tribulation Period, the Jewish nation will be refined and restored to God at its conclusion (Rom. 9:27; 11:26-32). They will recognize Jesus Christ as their Messiah (Zech. 12:10). Until then, the Lord Jesus Christ is building His Church which, although it includes both Jews and Gentiles, is chiefly composed of Gentiles. Moreover, God is bestowing blessings on Gentile believers to provoke the Jews to jealousy; this will ultimately result in their return to Him (Rom. 11:11-15). The Jews stumbled over Christ at His first advent and the blessing He offered them instead fell into the laps of the Gentiles, who were not even expecting it (Luke 20:9-16; Rom. 9:32). Thus, God is calling a people that were not His people by covenant to be His children (Hos. 2:23; Eph. 2:11-16). Gentiles are being brought into the good of the New Covenant (Hos. 1:10; Rom. 9:25-26).

There are those who teach that God is done with the nation of Israel and that the Church has replaced the nation of Israel in God's plan of blessing. However, it should be emphasized that the New Covenant, sealed by Christ's own blood, was not confirmed with Gentiles, but with the houses of Israel and Judah (Heb. 8:8). God has sworn by His own name to complete what He promised to Abraham, Isaac, Jacob, and David.

This truth was prophetically announced at the time of Christ's birth – He would be the one to achieve complete fulfillment of the Abrahamic Covenant (Luke 1:55). Simeon foretold that the infant Jesus Christ would be the revelation of God's goodness to the Gentiles and the glory of Israel (Luke 2:32). Anna proclaimed that He would bring redemption to Jerusalem (Luke 2:38). The priest Zechariah predicted that the Lord Jesus Christ would redeem His people, be a horn of salvation to Israel, deliver the Jews from all their enemies, and fulfill the covenant that God instituted with Abraham (Luke 1:67-80). *"My covenant I will not break, nor alter the word that has gone out of My lips"* (Ps. 89:34). Jehovah is a covenant-keeping God and through the two earthly advents of Christ, God will fulfill all that He has promised to do! Who but God could have ever devised a plan to show so much grace to rebels? Thankfully, Jew and Gentile can benefit from the New Covenant, which is sealed with the blood of the Lord Jesus Christ, at this very moment.

Israel's Future in Review

Many of the prophecies against the nations listed in Jeremiah 46-51 coincide with Israel's final spiritual refinement and restoration to God as detailed in Ezekiel 36-39, Daniel 7-8, Joel 2, and Zechariah 12-14. All these prophecies preview what is to come during and after the Tribulation Period. Believers in the Church Age should find of interest the events leading up to the fulfillment of these prophecies since the Church will be removed from the earth just prior to the beginning of the Tribulation Period.

Before the Kingdom Age commences, the Lord Jesus will descend to the earth to war against the Antichrist and his armies in the Megiddo Valley. His victory will deliver Jerusalem from the Antichrist's invading armies (Zech. 14). After the Battle of Armageddon, the nations will be gathered and judged (Matt. 13:47-50; 25:31-46); all those following the Antichrist will be killed (Rev. 19:20-21). Those who did not take his mark will be allowed to enter Christ's kingdom on earth. This will conclude the times of the Gentiles (Rom. 11:25; Rev. 11:1-2).

The Tribulation Period

God will judge the nations for their wickedness and refine and restore the Jewish nation to Himself during the seven-year Tribulation Period. There will be twenty-one specific judgments by God upon the earth. The Antichrist and the powers of darkness will also be rampant upon the earth, destroying and killing. In the book of Revelation, this horrific holocaust is quantified. In Revelation 6, we are told that one-fourth of the world's population will die from pestilence, war, and famine. Revelation 9 states that one third of mankind will be destroyed by fire. Two hundred million soldiers will be annihilated at the battle of Armageddon (Rev. 9:16). Moreover, in Revelation 7 and 13, we learn that an innumerable host of people from all nations will be martyred by the Beast for not worshipping him and receiving his mark.

If we understand the old Hebrew names correctly, Ezekiel 38 and 39 speak of Iraq, Iran, Egypt, Germany, and Turkey coming with Russia (*Rosh*) to attack Israel during the middle portion of the Tribulation Period. These armies will be annihilated by Christ's intervention through nature. A remnant will be allowed to escape to the north back into Russia (indicated as the land between the Black and Caspian Seas; see Joel 2:19-20). Zechariah 13:8-9 confirms that two-thirds of the Jews will die during the Tribulation Period. Only a small Jewish remnant will survive the refining fire of the Tribulation Period and be restored to God as His chosen people (Rom. 11). There will be numerous other judgments upon the earth that will also cause death and misery. The bottom line is that earth will not be the place to be during the Tribulation Period, as perhaps eighty percent of the world's population will perish.

Throughout the Tribulation Period, God, through His judgments, will take away from man what man has ignorantly claimed as his own. For example, natural man has labored, stolen, cheated, murdered, etc. in order to gain wealth, power, prestige, and sensual gratification. But conditions in this epic period of time will be such that death will be welcomed; even life's basic necessities of food and drinking water will be scarcely found (Rev. 6:6; 8:10-11). Both the prophet Isaiah and the apostle John describe the response of the wicked under the Lord's judgment at this time:

They shall go into the holes of the rocks, and into the caves of the earth, from the terror of the Lord and the glory of His majesty, when He arises to shake the earth mightily (Isa. 2:19).

Then the sky receded as a scroll when it is rolled up, and every mountain and island was moved out of its place. And the kings of the earth, the great men, the rich men, the commanders, the mighty men, every slave and every free man, hid themselves in the caves and in the rocks of the mountains, and said to the mountains and rocks, "Fall on us and hide us from the face of Him who sits on the throne and from the wrath of the Lamb! For the great day of His wrath has come, and who is able to stand?" (Rev. 6:14-17).

The Kingdom Age

By the end of the Tribulation Period, rebellious man will have nothing. God will demonstrate His control over all things and then purify the earth in order to usher in the Kingdom Age (Dan. 2:35, 44-45; Rom. 8:21). During this era, the earth and all its inhabitants will enjoy a thousand years of blessing under Christ's rule.

What will the Kingdom Age be like? From Isaiah 2:1-5 and 66:20, we learn that Jerusalem will be the religious center of the world. Christ will reign from there and all the nations will come there to praise, worship, and learn of Him. There will be no war or violence, only peace. All the earth will see the glory of the Lord Jesus. Isaiah 4:2-4 informs us that the Jews who live through the Tribulation will gaze upon Christ (the Branch of the Lord) and appreciate His splendor, glory, fruitfulness, and beauty. So great will be the glory of the Lord upon the earth that there will be no need for the sun or moon to illuminate it (Isa. 60:18-20).

At this time, strange phenomena in nature will be observed throughout the earth. The wolf and the lamb shall dwell together, as will the kid of the goat with the leopard, and the calf with the lion (Isa. 11:6-7). Small children shall play by the home of the asp and at the adder's den without being afraid (Isa. 11:8). The glory of the Lord will be displayed upon the world as abundantly as *"the waters cover the sea"* (Isa. 11:9). During the Kingdom Age, any nation opposing the Lord will be laid waste (Isa. 60:12). Longevity of life will be restored (Isa. 65:20).

These circumstances, though wonderful, should not be confused with the eternal state in which there is a new heaven and earth with no evil present (Isa. 65:17). Peter identifies the former as the Day of the Lord (2 Pet. 3:10), and the latter as the Day of God (2 Pet. 3:12). Peter also states that at the end of the Day of the Lord (i.e., at the end of Christ's millennial kingdom), the heavens and the earth shall pass away with a great noise and their elements shall melt with fervent heat and be burned up (2 Pet. 3:10). Isaiah states that *"all the host of heaven shall be dissolved, and the heavens shall be rolled up like a scroll"* (Isa. 34:4). He later foretells that after the millennial kingdom, God will create a new heaven and new earth (Isa. 65:17).

Following this creative feat, Paul states that there will be a divine audit to confirm that Christ has completely dealt with all sin and has restored creation to perfection and to its proper association with God. All the damage caused by sin will be corrected and then God will be all in all (1 Cor. 15:26-28). It is the writer's opinion that in the eternal state, previous distinctions such as Old Testament saints, the Church, Tribulation saints, the nation of Israel, etc. will be remembered, but not emphasized. These distinctions served God's purposes in time while He was unfolding His great plan of salvation in various stages, but will not be significant throughout eternity (1 Cor. 15:26-28; Rev. 21:24-27; 22:1-5).

There are several other clear distinctions between the Kingdom Age and the Eternal State, which those holding an amillennial viewpoint ignore. For example, the seas and oceans we know today will still be present during the Kingdom Age (Isa. 11:9; Ezek. 47:18; Zech. 14:8) but there will not be any seas in the new earth (Rev. 21:1). Likewise, geographic locations on earth today will exist in the Millennial Kingdom (Joel 3:18; Zech. 14:16-21) but obviously will not in the new earth. The new heaven and earth will not be created until after the Kingdom Age is concluded, Satan's last rebellion on earth is quelled (Rev. 20:7-10), and the planet we live on today is obliterated (Rev. 20:11; 2 Pet. 3:10).

Summary

Presently, the Lord sits on His Father's throne (Rev. 3:21). After the Church is with Christ in heaven, He will return to earth at the end of the Tribulation Period to defeat the Antichrist and his armies who have gathered to battle Israel (Zech. 14; Rev. 19). Shortly after this battle, Christ will separate those who are able to enter His kingdom from those who cannot; this is called the Judgment of Nations (Matt. 13:47-50; 25:31-47; Rev. 19:21). Then, the Lord Jesus will establish His righteous kingdom on the earth. Satan and demonic forces will be constrained within the bottomless pit during this one thousand-year period (Rev. 20:1-3) and the world will be governed by Christ from Jerusalem (Isa. 60:12-14; 66:10-14; Zech. 14:9). The curses that were placed on the earth in Adam's day will be lifted and the earth will be fully fruitful again (Ps. 72:16; Isa. 11:1-10; Rom. 8:18-22). Peace, prosperity, righteousness, justice, holiness, and the glory of God will be known throughout the planet.

What a blessing it will be when the curses that were put on the earth as a result of man's sin are lifted in the Kingdom Age (Rom. 8:21-22). A handful of seed casually scattered on a mountaintop will produce a great harvest (Ps. 72:16), longevity of life will be restored to humanity (Isa. 65:20), weapons will be used as agricultural implements (Mic. 4:3), and a spirit of peace and tranquility will rest upon the whole earth (Isa. 11:9). All this and more Christ shall do: *"Even so, come, Lord Jesus"* (Rev. 22:20)!

God Is Not Done With Israel

On the eve of His crucifixion, the Lord Jesus girded Himself with a towel, obtained a basin of water, and washed the twenty-four dirty feet of His disciples (John 13). They had been arguing among themselves as to who would be the greatest in the kingdom, so the Lord Jesus provided them with an example of how one works his or her way up in His kingdom – through humility and selfless service. The Lord then made this statement concerning the future reward of the faithful:

> *But you are those who have continued with Me in My trials. And I bestow upon you a kingdom, just as My Father bestowed one upon Me, that you may eat and drink at My table in My kingdom, and sit on thrones judging the twelve tribes of Israel* (Luke 22:28-30).

Just as the Lord Jesus Christ was destined to rule over all the nations in a future day, so surely would His disciples reign with Him over renewed Israel. The fact that the Lord Jesus mentions the existence of the twelve tribes of Israel within this kingdom ensures that He is not finished with the Jewish nation, as some teach. God has extended to the Jewish people a number of unconditional promises which He must fulfill, for God cannot lie (Titus 1:3).

The following is a sampling of the hundreds of Old Testament prophecies pertaining to the Jewish nation of Israel which have yet to be fulfilled:

1. The land given to Abraham has never been possessed by the Jews, but must be (Gen. 15:18). This land was to be possessed incrementally as based on the Jews' faithfulness to obey Jehovah and co-labor with Him in faith (Deut. 7:22; Josh 13:1; 21:43-44). But even during the glory days of David's and Solomon's reigns, the Jews

never controlled more than about ten percent of the inheritance promised to Abraham.

2. The Jews will start sacrificing again until the abomination of desolation, which occurs in the middle of the Tribulation Period (Dan. 9:27). At that time, the beast (Antichrist) will declare himself to be God and stop the Jewish sacrifices (2 Thess. 2:4-7). While on the earth, the Lord made mention of this prophecy as still being future (Matt. 24). It has not been fulfilled since that time.

3. Jerusalem will be the worship center of the earth during the millennium. All nations will come to Jerusalem to see the glory of God (Isa. 2:1-4; 60:14; 66:10-18; Zech. 14:16-21).

4. The Jews will be highly esteemed by all Gentiles during the millennial reign of Christ (Isa. 60:12-15; Zech. 8:20-23). This worldwide favor for the Jewish people has never been realized.

5. The Jewish nation will be restored to Jehovah. Though the prophecies predicting a political rebirth have recently been fulfilled (e.g. Ezek. 37:15-20; Isa. 11:13; 66:8), the nation has yet to experience spiritual rebirth (Joel 3). This will occur at the end of the Tribulation Period.

6. As a disciplinary action, God began scattering the Jews throughout the nations in 722 BC with the invasion of Israel by the Assyrians. He will completely gather all Jews back to the land of Israel at the close of the Tribulation Period (Ezek. 39:28-29).

7. After the Jews regain the land of Israel by the sword (war), they will experience a period of false peace under the Antichrist (Dan. 9:27).

8. Towards the end of the first half of the Tribulation Period, the armies of Russia, Iraq, Iran, Egypt, and Turkey will attack the Jews, but God will protect Israel from this invasion by raining down large

hail stones, heavy rain, pestilence, and even fire from heaven (Ezek. 38-39).

9. By the end of the Tribulation Period, the Jewish nation will receive a new heart and be indwelt by the Holy Spirit (Ezek. 36:17-26; Joel 2:18-28; Isa. 32; Isa. 44:1-6). This will begin with the sealing of the 144,000 Jews in the early portion of the Tribulation Period (Rev. 7).

10. The battle of Armageddon is yet future, but will not happen until Israel is back in the Promised Land, including the Golan Heights (Joel 3; Zech. 12; 14).

11. Babylon will be completely destroyed by fire and made uninhabitable. This could not happen until the Jews were dwelling in Bashan (the Golan Heights), as they are today (Jer. 50).

12. Only after the adulterous nation of Israel repents and receives Jesus Christ as Messiah in the "latter days" will the kingdom of David be established (Hosea 3:1-5; Zech. 12:1-10). This was Jehovah's unconditional promise to David (1 Chron. 17:12).

13. A resurrection of faithful Jews will accompany the spiritual restoration of the Jewish nation (Isa. 26:8, 18-21).

14. God will restore Israel, the adulterous wife, and He will protect her from harm, though all nations will oppose her during the Tribulation Period (Isa. 54; Jer. 30:7; Rev. 12:13-17). Those Jews surviving this terrible holocaust will enter Christ's kingdom (Isa. 4:2).

15. During the millennial kingdom of Christ, the faithful from the Gentile nations will gather with the Jewish nation to honor Christ at Jerusalem (Isa. 11:1-11; Isa. 60; 65:18-25; Rev. 21).

16. During the millennial kingdom, a temple with specific dimensions will be built in Jerusalem (Ezek. 40-43). This temple has never existed.

17. During the millennial kingdom, the twelve tribes will receive specific land allotments within the region promised Abraham (Ezek. 47-48). These specific allocations have never occurred.

18. Romans 11 declares that God has always maintained a pure Jewish remnant to honor Him. Today, this remnant is a portion of the Church but when the times of the Gentiles are over, the blindness of the Jewish nation, which resulted from rejecting Christ, will end. Then the entire nation will be a purified remnant never to depart from the Lord again (Isa. 4). The prophet Ezekiel plainly describes this future reality:

> And He said to me, "Son of man, this is the place of My throne and the place of the soles of My feet, where I will dwell in the midst of the children of Israel forever. No more shall the house of Israel defile My holy name, they nor their kings, by their harlotry or with the carcasses of their kings on their high places. When they set their threshold by My threshold, and their doorpost by My doorpost, with a wall between them and Me, they defiled My holy name by the abominations which they committed; therefore I have consumed them in My anger. Now let them put their harlotry and the carcasses of their kings far away from Me, and I will dwell in their midst forever" (Ezek. 43:7-9).

Clearly Jehovah, through the prophets of old, has declared His future plans for the Jewish nation. All these unfilled prophecies indicate the Messiah is coming again and that Jehovah is not finished with His covenant people. The prophet Isaiah declares that in a future day, once idolatrous Israel is restored to the Lord in purity, the wealth and honor of the nations will be theirs. At that time, the Jews' relation with Christ will serve as a beacon to draw all men to Him also.

> Thus says the Lord: "The labor of Egypt and merchandise of Cush and of the Sabeans, men of stature, shall come over to you, and they shall be yours; they shall walk behind you, they shall come over in chains; and they shall bow down to you. They will make supplication to you, saying, 'Surely God is in you, and there is no other; there is no other God.'" Truly You are God, who hide Yourself, O God of Israel, the Savior! They shall be ashamed and also disgraced, all of them; they shall go in confusion together, who are makers of idols.

But Israel shall be saved by the Lord with an everlasting salvation; you shall not be ashamed or disgraced forever and ever. For thus says the Lord, who created the heavens, who is God, who formed the earth and made it, who has established it, who did not create it in vain, who formed it to be inhabited: "I am the Lord, and there is no other. I have not spoken in secret, in a dark place of the earth; I did not say to the seed of Jacob, 'Seek Me in vain'; I, the Lord, speak righteousness, I declare things that are right. Assemble yourselves and come; draw near together, you who have escaped from the nations. They have no knowledge, who carry the wood of their carved image, and pray to a god that cannot save. Tell and bring forth your case; yes, let them take counsel together. Who has declared this from ancient time? Who has told it from that time? Have not I, the Lord? And there is no other God besides Me, a just God and a Savior; there is none besides Me. Look to Me, and be saved, all you ends of the earth! For I am God, and there is no other" (Isa. 45:14-22; also see Isa. 62:1-7).

The prophet Jeremiah wonderfully summarizes Jehovah's love for His covenant people and His future intentions to restore the Jews to their Promised Land and then personally dwell and commune with them forever afterwards:

Behold, I will gather them out of all countries where I have driven them in My anger, in My fury, and in great wrath; I will bring them back to this place, and I will cause them to dwell safely. They shall be My people, and I will be their God; then I will give them one heart and one way, that they may fear Me forever, for the good of them and their children after them. And I will make an everlasting covenant with them, that I will not turn away from doing them good; but I will put My fear in their hearts so that they will not depart from Me. Yes, I will rejoice over them to do them good, and I will assuredly plant them in this land, with all My heart and with all My soul. For thus says the Lord: "Just as I have brought all this great calamity on this people, so I will bring on them all the good that I have promised them" (Jer. 32:37-42).

God's proven longsuffering, merciful, compassionate nature towards Israel should be of immense encouragement to the Church. First, through Israel's rejection of it, the message of grace in Christ came to the Gentiles. Second, God's present dealings with Israel should encourage the Church to better prepare herself for the Marriage Supper of the Lamb, which occurs in heaven and prior to Israel's being restored to Jehovah. Third, God demonstrates that He always keeps His promises, even when it pains Him to do so. Clearly, God's sovereignty and foreknowledge cooperate to ensure mankind God's utmost blessing while at the same time ensuring the highest honor to His name. The Lord God is all in all!

In contemplation of the vast treasury of Old Testament prophecies, it is quite obvious that Israel does have the hope of glory. We agree with the prophet Isaiah's assessment of the Kingdom Age: *"In that day the Lord of hosts will be for a crown of glory and a diadem of beauty to the remnant of His people"* (Isa. 28:5). Israel's only hope is centered in the second coming of their Messiah, the Lord Jesus Christ!

O Israel, hope in the Lord; for with the Lord there is mercy, and with Him is abundant redemption. And He shall redeem Israel from all his iniquities (Ps. 130:7-8).

The Church's Hope – The Rapture

Similar, but Different

As mentioned in the *Preface*, many holding to reformed or covenant theology believe that God is finished with the Jewish nation, and that the Church is now Israel. As the reader may not be familiar with these doctrinal movements, a brief discussion is warranted to enhance our evaluation of eschatological views held by these theological systems.

Covenant and Reformed Theology

Renald Showers defines covenant theology "as a system ... which attempts to develop the Bible's philosophy of history on the basis of two or three covenants. It represents the whole of Scripture and history as being covered by two or three covenants."[1] It is noted that none of these covenants are specifically mentioned in the Bible. Charles Ryrie summarizes these supposed covenants:

> Formal definitions of covenant theology are not easy to find even in the writings of covenant theologians. Most of the statements that pass for definitions are in fact descriptions or characterizations of the system. The article in *Bakers Dictionary of Theology* comes close to a definition when it says that covenant theology is distinguished by "the place it gives to the covenants" because it "represents the whole of Scripture as being covered by covenants: (1) the covenant of works, and (2) the covenant of grace." This is an accurate description of the covenant system. Covenant theology is a system of theology based on the two covenants of works and grace as governing categories for the understanding of the entire Bible.

> In covenant theology the covenant of works is said to be an agreement between God and Adam promising life to Adam for perfect obedience and including death as the penalty for failure. But Adam sinned and thus mankind failed to meet the requirements of the

101

covenant of works. Therefore, a second covenant, the covenant of grace, was brought into operation. Louis Berkhof defines it as "that gracious agreement between the offended God and the offending but elect sinner, in which God promises salvation through faith in Christ, and the sinner accepts this believingly, promising a life of faith and obedience."

Some Reformed theologians have introduced a third covenant, the covenant of redemption. It was made in eternity past and became the basis for the covenant of grace, just described, between God and the elect. This covenant of redemption is supposed to be "the agreement between the Father, giving the Son as Head and Redeemer of the elect, and the Son, voluntarily taking the place of those whom the Father had given him." These two or three covenants become the core and bases of operation for covenant theology in its interpretation of the Scriptures.[2]

Yet the divine revelations to Israel and the Church were different and remain diverse. The Church is to declare the gospel of grace to the masses. The Lord and His disciples preached the gospel of the kingdom, that it's the coming of a literal, earthly, political kingdom in Israel (Matt. 4:17). Furthermore, a failure to draw a distinction between the unconditional covenant which God instituted with Abraham and the conditional covenant confirmed with Moses at Sinai, places the Church under the Mosaic Law. Paul adamantly refutes this idea in his letter to the Galatian believers:

And this I say, that the law, which was four hundred and thirty years later, cannot annul the covenant that was confirmed before by God in Christ, that it should make the promise of no effect. For if the inheritance is of the law, it is no longer of promise; but God gave it to Abraham by promise (Gal. 3:17-18).

The Gentiles were never under the Law, so Paul warns that they should not put themselves under it (Gal. 3:25; 5:3-4). The Law does not achieve spiritual perfection for us; the Law reveals our imperfections and sin (Rom. 3:20). The message of the book of Hebrews to the Jews is: In Christ, you have been delivered from the Law through a superior sacrifice, covenant, and priesthood. Do not put yourself back under what only condemned (Heb. 2:1-3; 10:38).

Accordingly, those holding a covenant or reformed theological framework generally believe that God only has one people, one plan for them, and one means of saving them with the ultimate goal of bringing His people into His eternal presence. This position often combines both Law keeping and grace in Christ as needed aspects of achieving or maintaining salvation. According to this view, the Church contains all believers from Adam on and was not created at Pentecost by the Holy Spirit. The ongoing saga of all human existence is pessimistically understood as good and evil continuing to develop, both struggling side by side until divine catastrophic judgment suddenly terminates evil, at which point, eternity begins. This perception means that the Jewish nation is cursed by God and the Church will ultimately receive what God has promised Israel.

There Is a Difference

In the previous section, many of the yet unfulfilled and unconditional promises of God to the Jewish people were reviewed. The Jews failed to keep the Law but Jehovah established a new covenant with the house of Israel and Judah which was sealed with His own Son's blood in order to complete that which He swore He would do for them. The Law was instituted to show His people that they were sinners, that they could not save themselves, and that they needed a Savior (Gal. 3:24).

Through the New Covenant, Jehovah will righteously fulfill all His previous promises to His covenant people, despite their past failures. Though the Church (mainly composed of Gentiles) becomes a second benefactor of this covenant (Rom. 11:16-26; Eph. 3:6-9), a distinction between the Jewish nation and the Church is upheld throughout the New Testament (e.g., 1 Cor. 10:32) to guard against a wrong understanding of God's plan for Israel. In fact, the Church will reign with Christ in the Kingdom Age and judge the twelve tribes of Israel, but the Jews will also have a position of honor among the nations at this time (Zech. 8:22-23; Luke 22:30).

There are some aspects of the New Covenant which both Israel and the Church share. For example, both are referred to as a "called out company." But this would be true of any of God's people in any dispensation of God's work – the Lord's people are citizens of heaven living on earth and are to represent Him as His ambassadors (2 Cor. 5:20; Phil. 3:20; Heb. 11:13). Like Abraham, God's people in any age are to be pilgrims and strangers as they journey heavenward. With that said, Scripture declares many more distinctions between Israel and the Church than similarities. For example:

- The Church is referred to as a mystery of God that was not revealed until after Christ's ascension, but Israel was spoken of in detail throughout the Old Testament (Eph. 3:5-9).
- Israel began with Abraham, but the Church began at Pentecost (Acts 2; Gen. 12).
- The Jewish nation existed in Christ's day, but He spoke of the Church in the future tense (Matt. 16:18).
- One is physically born into Israel, but one must be spiritually reborn to be in the Church (1 Cor. 12:12).
- Christ is the head of the Church, while Abraham is the head of Israel (Eph. 5:23; Gen. 15:3-5).
- Those in the Church have a heavenly citizenship; however, those in Israel have an earthly citizenship (Phil. 3:20; Ezek. 36:24-26; 39:28-29; Zech. 8:20-23).
- There is no difference between the Jews and the Gentiles in the Church, but Gentiles are despised by and have no part in Israel (Eph. 2:13-17; 3:6; Gal. 3:28).
- The Church is the bride of Christ and is destined to rule and reign with Him, yet Christ is the king of Israel (2 Tim. 2:12; Isa. 44:6; Eph. 5:24-25).
- Israel had a chosen tribe (descendants of Aaron) to be their priests on earth; however, the Church is completely composed of a holy, royal priesthood which offers heavenly sacrifices (Heb. 7:5; 9:7; 10:19-22; 1 Pet. 2:1-9).
- The Church will be taken to heaven via rapture and then will rule with Christ during His one-thousand-year reign after the Tribulation Period, but Israel will be converted during the Tribulation Period and will then be earthly subjects of Christ (1 Thess. 4:13-18; Zech. 12:8-10; 14:1-9).

Clearly, a theological distinction between the Jewish nation and the Church is maintained throughout the Bible, at least through the Millennial Kingdom (i.e., Rev. 20). The following figure graphically portrays God's plan of salvation for Israel and the Church.

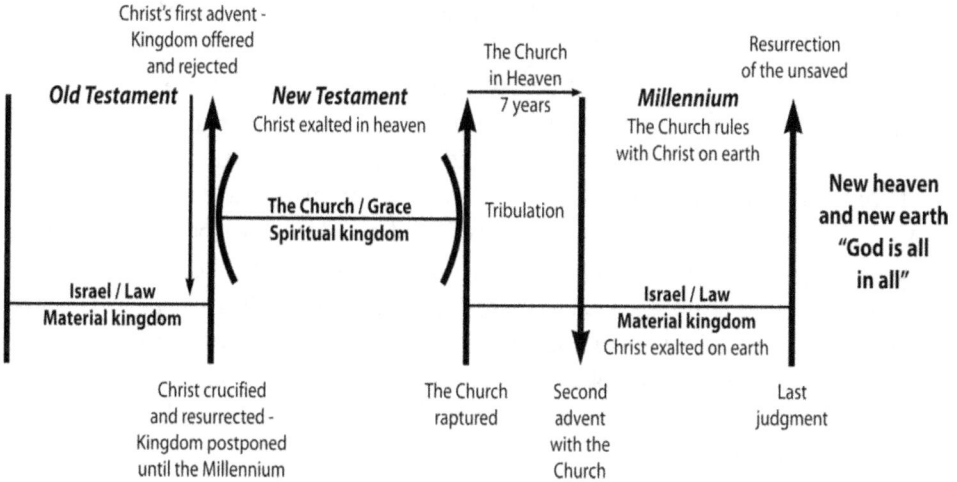

GOD'S SALVATION FOR ISRAEL AND THE CHURCH

Christ's first advent - Kingdom offered and rejected

The Church in Heaven

Resurrection of the unsaved

Old Testament

New Testament
Christ exalted in heaven

7 years

Millennium
The Church rules with Christ on earth

The Church / Grace
Spiritual kingdom

Tribulation

New heaven and new earth "God is all in all"

Israel / Law
Material kingdom

Israel / Law
Material kingdom
Christ exalted on earth

Christ crucified and resurrected - Kingdom postponed until the Millennium

The Church raptured

Second advent with the Church

Last judgment

The broadest spiritual division among people living on the earth at any time would be saints and the lost – those who have been justified in Christ and those who have not been. Yet the New Testament clearly identifies three human subcategories which anticipates the future working of God. Paul instructs believers to *"give no offense, either to the Jews or the Gentiles or to the Church of God"* (1 Cor. 10:32). The unconverted nation of Israel and unregenerate Gentiles were not to be stumbled from hearing the gospel. Quoting Amos and Peter, James explains that God has a different plan for saving Gentiles than He does for restoring the Jewish nation:

Simon has declared how God at the first visited the Gentiles to take out of them a people for His name. And with this the words of the prophets agree, just as it is written: "After this I will return and will rebuild the tabernacle of David, which has fallen down; I will rebuild its ruins, and I will set it up; so that the rest of mankind may seek the

Lord, even all the Gentiles who are called by My name, says the Lord who does all these things" (Acts 15:14-17).

Jehovah would call a people His children that were not His people (Hos. 2:23), then He would rebuild the Jewish nation to become a beacon of divine truth among the nations (Amos 9:11-12). This is why Paul was so zealous to share the gospel with his fellow countrymen: *"Brethren, my heart's desire and prayer to God for Israel is that they may be saved"* (Rom. 10:1). He knew Israel's future, but it was not to be in His lifetime.

Presently, God is calling to Himself a people (Gentiles) that had no hope and no God (Eph. 2:11). When the Church is complete, the Lord Jesus shall descend to the clouds and with a trump and a shout gather all that are His from the earth. This will happen in the twinkling of an eye (1 Thess. 4:13-18; 1 Cor. 15:51-52). Then He shall begin to spiritually refine and awaken the Jewish nation and, after their conversion, establish the throne of David forever. While the Church is vertically raptured to meet Christ in the clouds prior to the Tribulation (1 Thess. 4:13-18), all Jews worldwide will be gathered horizontally back to the land of Israel to worship Him there at the end of the Tribulation Period (Ezek. 39:28-29).

Old Testament Pictures

God's plan for dealing with Gentiles and the Jewish nation can be seen in seed form all the way back in Genesis. Through a dream, God spoke to Jacob and reconfirmed the covenant He had made with Abraham and Isaac. Jacob was promised seed that would be as the dust of the earth (Gen. 28:14). Isaac was promised descendants as numerous as the stars of heaven (Gen. 26:4). Abraham, in whom the covenant was established, was promised both (Gen. 22:17). Why the difference? Because two different peoples are being alluded to: an earthly people ("as the dust of the earth") and a heavenly people ("as the stars of heaven"). Isaac represents the resurrected Christ who has ascended into heaven to obtain His inheritance, and Jacob represents the expansion of the nation of Israel, which will inherit an earthly land during the Millennium.

Isaac only took one bride, Rebecca. She pictures the Church. By a marriage covenant, she was secured as a bride from a faraway land without knowing her espoused husband. They laid eyes on each other for the first time in a field between the land from where she was called and her new home. Then they returned to Isaac's home as man and wife (Gen. 24:57-67). This is beautiful typology representing the calling of a Gentile bride for Christ and their first meeting, in the clouds, before going to their heavenly abode.

Stephen, while preaching to the Sanhedrin in Acts 7, declared that prophetic patterns imprinted within the lives of the Patriarchs were given to us as an example to learn from. Stephen told them that neither Joseph nor Moses had been accepted when they were first presented to their brethren as king and deliverer, respectively. But the second time, Joseph's brethren acknowledged their brother as king and their wrong in selling him into slavery. Also, Moses, on his second presentation, was accepted as the deliverer. Both Joseph and Moses married Gentile women; they did not take Jewish wives. By reviewing the lives of Joseph and Moses, Stephen asserted that God foreknew that the Jewish nation would reject His Son at the first advent but after Christ received a Gentile bride (the Church), they would trust Him at His second advent. When Stephen drew the analogy to its biblical climax, the Jewish leaders could not tolerate the truth any longer and murdered him.

Summary

All of God's promises to the Church and the nation of Israel find their fulfillment in the Lord Jesus Christ (2 Cor. 1:20). However, Scripture reveals that God has chosen various means of extending His grace to those exercising faith in His Word throughout the human timeline. Accordingly, the message and promises bestowed to Israel are quite different than those entrusted to the Church. Distinctive promises prompt specific expectations for the future. While the Church can certainly rejoice with Israel with respect to Christ's coming millennial kingdom, the Church's hope centers in events preceding it. Paul confirms that the three chief Christian virtues are faith, hope, and love. With the rapture of the Church, faith and hope will have exhausted themselves (1 Cor. 13:8, 13). Once the Church is with Christ, all that faith suffered for and all that hope expectantly longed for will have been achieved, and then the redeemed will bask in the love of God forever – for *"love never fails."*

The writer of Hebrews acknowledges this strong connection between the believer's faith and hope and that both have their culmination in Christ's coming for the Church. *"For yet a little while, and He who is coming will come and will not tarry. Now the just shall live by faith"* (Heb. 10:37-38). Although Scripture repeatedly emphasizes hope in the Christian experience, many believers today unfortunately do not know what their hope is. Some loathe the future and live in fear of it. This was not the disposition of the apostles, who lived out their lives exuberantly for Christ because they anticipated their future with joy and excitement. Regrettably, much of the Church maintains a dismal outlook rather than a blessed hope, and thus are not influenced by it. A lack of compassion for the poor and needy and no remorse for perishing souls are symptoms of misplaced hope. Fear creates bondage, but hope liberates the redeemed soul to serve with joy (Heb. 2:15). So what is the Church's hope?

What Is the Church's Hope?

It is common to hear someone respond to the question, "Would you go to heaven if you died today?" with a squeamish "Well, I hope so." Whether or not such an individual is actually saved or not only the Lord knows, but what is evident is that the responder has no assurance of salvation. This is a matter that John wrote to alleviate: *"These things I have written to you who believe in the name of the Son of God, that you may know that you have eternal life"* (1 Jn. 5:13). Thus, a true believer will gain understanding of the salvation that he or she possesses in Christ by studying and trusting in what Scripture proclaims about their security in Christ. This assurance of salvation (i.e., the helmet of salvation) guards the believer's mind against despair during arduous times because his or her eternal future with Christ in heaven is secure no matter what happens on earth.

Believers are therefore not hoping that they will be saved from God's judgment of their sin, for Christ has already been judged in their place. Rather, believers are to know that they are eternally secure in Christ (John 5:24) and long with anticipation for the conclusion of their salvation – glorification. Presently, they can rejoice that their souls are saved from the penalty of sin, that through the Holy Spirit they have power over sin, but are to continue to anticipate a future day when they will be saved from the presence of sin. At that moment a believer's body will be transformed into holy humanity, nothing of the flesh nature inherited from Adam will remain, and he or she will be removed from the presence of sin (i.e., from the corruption of the world).

Hope, in the biblical sense, is therefore defined as "having present joy in the future promises of God," a meaning borne out by the New Testament Greek words rendered as "hope." *Elpis* occurs eighty-six times in the New Testament and is translated "hope" all but once (it is rendered "faith" in Heb. 10:23). Its verb form *elpizo* is translated "hope" fourteen of thirty-two occurrences in the New Testament; all the remaining occurrences are rendered as some form of "trusting." On-ly *elpis* and *elpizo* are translated "hope" in the portion of the New Testament pertaining to the Church Age (Acts to Revelation). Therefore, when Christians "hope" in something, it means they are "anticipating something with confidence." The believer's hope is thus living, and allows him or her to have present joy in the future promises of God. Thankfully, *hope* as it relates to the various tenses of our salvation in Christ (past, present, and future) is a "know so expectation," rather than a "hope so possibility." The believer's calling in Christ is completely fostered in assurance, especially the final call home.

The believer walking hand in hand with Christ is invincible and immortal until his or her work on earth is done. At that time, the helmet of salvation, the shield of faith, and the breastplate of righteousness will hit the floor with a clang, for the battle days will be over and eternal rest will begin. Certainly, many believers who were waiting for the Lord's return have already been called home to heaven through the doorway of death.

Our flesh nature wants its own way for as long as it can have it, but death is a barrier which decisively ends its influence in our lives. Hence, our fallen nature does not want to think about death. In fact, the brevity of life would serve to motivate the flesh to indulge itself with worldly pleasures all the more. Yet, after His victory at Calvary, Christ broke through death and provided us with a way into God's presence (Heb. 6:18-20). The fact that He has been resurrected ensures that all those in Him will be resurrected also in a future day. If believers die before their glorification at Christ's coming, then they can be confident that their souls will immediately be in Christ's presence in heaven (2 Cor. 5:8).

Christ is presently with us on earth; in the future, we shall be with Him in heaven. His forever abiding presence with us is certain, though our intimacy with Him now depends on our desire for it. With his own execution looming, Paul conveyed his assurance of these truths to his spiritual son Timothy.

> *For I am already being poured out as a drink offering, and the time of my departure is at hand. I have fought the good fight, I have fin-ished the race, I have kept the faith. Finally, there is laid up for me the crown of righteousness, which the Lord, the righteous Judge, will*

give to me on that Day, and not to me only but also to all who have loved His appearing (2 Tim. 4:6-8).

We also would do well to live each and every day with the anticipation of Christ's coming. There is a reward for those who do, and our lives will be more joyful and fruitful in light of the imminent expectation.

When the Lord saves a repentant sinner, He completely redeems that person's spirit, soul, and body (1 Cor. 6:20; 1 Thess. 5:23). The soul and the spirit are immediately delivered from the *penalty* of sin when one confesses his or her sinfulness before God and accepts Christ's free gift of salvation (Rom. 10:9). After this, God continues to cleanse defilement from the believer's life; this progressive work is called "sanctification," and in the practical sense, this saves the soul from the *power* of sin. The body, however, is not saved from the *presence* of sin until it experiences a complete overhaul called glorification. This aspect of salvation is what Paul referred to when he wrote, *"For now our salvation is nearer than when we first believed"* (Rom. 13:11).

All believers will experience this transformation simultaneously at the coming of the Lord Jesus for His Church. Paul wrote the believers at Thessalonica of this event shortly after their conversion:

> *For the Lord Himself will descend from heaven with a shout, with the voice of an archangel, and with the trumpet of God. And the dead in Christ will rise first. Then we who are alive and remain shall be caught up together with them in the clouds to meet the Lord in the air. And thus we shall always be with the Lord. Therefore comfort one another with these words* (1 Thess. 4:16-17).

In a twinkling of an eye, what was corruptible will be incorruptible, and what was mortal will be immortal (1 Cor. 15:51-52). The Greek verb *harpazo* is translated "caught up" in the above passage. This word means "to snatch up with force." It used in John 10:12 to describe the powerful and sudden attack of a wolf on unsuspecting sheep. The believer's body will be instantly transformed and translated with immense divine power. Though not a biblical term, the Church often refers to this event as "the rapture." "Rapture" is a bit easier to roll off the tongue than saying "harpazo." Rapture also conveys the thought of powerful transportation of something in the English language. At the Rapture of the Church, sin and pain will cease to exist within all believers in the Church. The believer's glorified body will be enabled to worship and to please God without any hindrance of the flesh or any ills of its previously fallen state.

Paul had one hope (Eph. 4:4), one earnest expectation, the *blessed hope*: *"Looking for the blessed hope and glorious appearing of our great God and Savior Jesus Christ"* (Titus 2:13). While this may include aspects of Christ's future kingdom as well, it is noted that the believer's faith and hope finish their course at Christ's coming for the Church (the rapture), yet love, as previously mentioned, continues forever (1 Cor. 13:8, 13). Paul had lived each and every day in the anticipation of being imminently brought into the presence of Christ:

> *According to my earnest expectation and hope that in nothing I shall be ashamed, but with all boldness, as always, so now also Christ will be magnified in my body, whether by life or by death. For to me, to live is Christ, and to die is gain. But if I live on in the flesh, this will mean fruit from my labor; yet what I shall choose I cannot tell. For I am hard-pressed between the two, having a desire to depart and be with Christ, which is far better* (Phil. 1:20-23).

Although Paul yearned to be with the Lord, as long as the Lord had work for him to do he would remain on earth to perform it. He understood that his ministry was needful for the Church; thus, he pressed onward until the Lord would call him home, either through death or through glorification at Christ's coming for the Church. Beloved, this is the pattern that each believer is to follow.

The Church is not to be waiting for the Antichrist to appear, but for Christ Himself to translate them from the earth into heaven. The Church is not waiting for the inhabitants of earth to be slaughtered during the Tribulation Period, but rather longs to be removed from this wicked world to be with Christ. While the Church is to be evangelical until the Lord's return, it is understood that He alone will cleanse wickedness from the world and establish His throne in Jerusalem – we are not preparing the Kingdom for Him.

Many of the eschatological views that the Church is embracing today incite fear, rather than hope. Much of the Lord's teaching in the latter weeks of His earthly ministry was to instill hope in His disciples; He was not trying to discourage them from pressing on to their Higher Calling (Phil. 3:13-14). They were to watch and wait for His return, while diligently laboring for those who would trust Him for salvation (Matt. 28:19-20). As Christ has yet to return for His Church, both the great commission and the blessed hope are to remain in the foremost thinking of every believer's mind. This is why the Lord Jesus, on the eve of His crucifixion, after telling His disciples that He was leaving them, could console their fears with these words:

> *Let not your heart be troubled; you believe in God, believe also in Me. In My Father's house are many mansions; if it were not so, I would have told you. I go to prepare a place for you. And if I go and prepare a place for you, I will come again and receive you to Myself; that where I am, there you may be also* (John 14:1-3).

What is the blessed hope of the Church? The imminent coming of the Lord Jesus Christ to the air to suddenly gather up His Church from the earth to be with Him in glory. This is part of the "First Resurrection." The anticipation of bodily resurrection and glorification is indeed a living hope! It is a purifying hope that should consecrate and sanctify each day of a believer's life. However, not all Christians have this hope; many hold an eschatological view of the coming Millennial Kingdom or of the Rapture of the Church that is anything but hopeful. Before reviewing various eschatological views, an understanding of what the Bible teaches about the resurrection is needful. There are two resurrections of the dead identified in Scripture and these become the milestones within each eschatological view.

Two Resurrections

It is quite possible that Job is the oldest book in our Bibles, and, ironically, it is the first to speak of resurrection. Scripture declares that Job *"was blameless and upright, and one that feared God, and shunned evil"* (Job 1:1). He was an honorable man who suffered greatly for the glory of God and for personal refinement. Even after the loss of all his wealth, his children, and his health, Job would not blaspheme God, but instead anticipated being with Him in the afterlife:

> *For I know that my Redeemer lives, and He shall stand at last on the earth; and after my skin is destroyed, this I know, that in my flesh I shall see God, whom I shall see for myself, and my eyes shall behold, and not another. How my heart yearns within me!* (Job 19:25-27).

Even if God took Job's life, he understood that he would be resurrected in a future day and that he would dwell with his Redeemer. Though Job suffered greatly, God did restore and bless him later in his life (Job 42). What was his hope during those difficult days? He knew that his resurrected body would not be covered with sores, but would fully prepare him to be with his God.

Natural law governs us while we sojourn on earth, but that is not true in the spiritual realm of the afterlife. Whether one spends eternity in heaven or in hell, everyone will undergo a spiritual resurrection. This ensures that all individuals will have a body suited for their final destination. The Lord Jesus taught that He, as the Son of God, created all life and that all life was in Him (John 1:3-4). He also stated that at His command all the deceased would be resurrected (i.e., every disembodied soul would be joined to an immortal body that can never die):

> *Most assuredly, I say to you, he who hears My word and believes in Him who sent Me has everlasting life, and shall not come into judgment, but has passed from death into life. Most assuredly, I say to*

you, the hour is coming, and now is, when the dead will hear the voice of the Son of God; and those who hear will live. For as the Father has life in Himself, so He has granted the Son to have life in Himself, and has given Him authority to execute judgment also, because He is the Son of Man. Do not marvel at this; for the hour is coming in which all who are in the graves will hear His voice and come forth – those who have done good, to the resurrection of life, and those who have done evil, to the resurrection of condemnation (John 5:24-29).

From this passage we learn that there will be two types of resurrection: a resurrection of the just to enable eternal residence in heaven and a resurrection of the condemned to be punished for eternity in the Lake of Fire (Rev. 20:10, 15). The Lord Jesus has received authority from His Father to initiate both of these resurrections, but Scripture informs us that the first resurrection (i.e., of the just) occurs in several stages, while the resurrection of the condemned happens all at once.

Timing of the Resurrections

Though the resurrection of the condemned occurs all at once at the Great White Throne judgment (Rev. 20:11-15), the *resurrection of life*, also called the *first resurrection* (Rev. 20:5-6), occurs for the righteous at several distinct points in time prior to the Great White Throne judgment. The Eternal State, the everlasting reality of a new heaven and new earth without sin, follows this final judgment. Time ceases to have meaning after this. Christ was raised from the dead three days after He gave His life as a ransom for humanity at Calvary. Though there had been six bodily resurrections recorded in the Bible previously, Christ was the first individual to experience glorification (to receive a glorified body which would be suitable for the dynamics of heaven). The number seven is used in the Bible to symbolize completeness and perfection and Christ, the seventh human raised from the dead, was the first to experience perfect resurrection; as Paul puts it, the Lord Jesus was *"the first fruits of the dead"* to appear before God in heaven (1 Cor. 15:20-23).

Shortly after Christ's resurrection, some deceased believers were also raised from the dead, probably as further validation of Christ's own resurrection. They either underwent a bodily resurrection (like

116

Lazarus' resurrection recorded in John 12) or glorification (the same type of resurrection that Christ experienced) – Scripture does not specify which type. If this were only a bodily resurrection, those saints would have had to die a second time. It seems unlikely that God would have allowed these saints to enjoy fellowship with Christ in paradise and then put them back on the earth again to live a normal human existence in a sin-cursed world.

The next stage of the first resurrection will be when Christ returns for His Church. He will descend into the clouds and all true believers (both those who have died and also those still alive) will be quickly caught up from the earth to experience glorification (1 Thess. 4:13-18; 1 Cor. 15:51-52). At that moment, all Christians (and perhaps Old Testament saints as well, per Heb. 11:39-40) will receive the same kind of perfect body that the Lord did after His resurrection (Phil. 3:21; 1 Jn. 3:2). This spectacular event ends the Church Age and will be followed by a devastating period on earth called the Tribulation.

After all true Christians (i.e., those who had been born again and are indwelt by God) have been removed from the earth, the Antichrist will be allowed to rule the world for seven years (2 Thess. 2:4-7; Dan. 9:27). God will pour out great wrath upon the earth at this time and Satan will attempt to gain as many followers as possible and slaughter those who will not take his mark and pledge allegiance to the Antichrist (Rev. 12:12; 13:11-18). The holocaust of life during this time will be horrendous; the Lord Jesus said that if He should tarry longer than the appointed time for His return to the earth, humanity would be wiped out (Matt. 24:21-22). Considering the twenty-one specific divine judgments which occur at this time (Rev. 6-17), the Battle of Gog and Magog (Ezek. 38 - 39), the chastening of Israel (Rom. 9:27), and the Battle of Armageddon (Rev. 19), it is quite conceivable that seventy-five percent of the world population will die during this epoch. Two-thirds of all Jews will be murdered during the Tribulation Period (Zech. 13:7-8), but God will protect a remnant of His covenant people from the Antichrist (Rev. 12:13-17) in order to fulfill remaining promises to Abraham and David (Gen. 15:18-21; Ps. 89:3-4; Luke 1:32-33, 67-79).

The good news is that many will choose to be beheaded by the Antichrist (Rev. 20:4) rather than take his mark of identification and worship him (Rev. 7:9-14). Those who heard the gospel message of Jesus

Christ during the Church Age will not be given the opportunity to receive salvation during the Tribulation Period – they will take *"the mark of the beast"* and follow him into destruction (2 Thess. 2:10-12). Because they rejected God's Son's offer of salvation and opted instead to pursue pleasure in unrighteousness, God will not allow them to understand the truth in order to be saved. On the other hand, those martyred for choosing to worship God rather than the Antichrist will experience the first resurrection at the end of the Tribulation Period (Rev. 20:4). This miraculous event coincides with Christ's physical return to the earth to destroy the Antichrist, to judge and remove wickedness from the earth, and to establish His earthly kingdom, which will last one thousand years (Rev. 20:4-6).

Revelation 20:1-8 informs us that Satan will be bound in the bottomless pit during Christ's reign on earth. However, at the end of that time he will be released to again test man's resolve to follow God. Even after one thousand years of peace and prosperity, the devil will successfully deceive the nations of the earth to rebel against Christ. One might ask, "Why would God allow Satan to lead such a rebellion against His own Son? Why not just destroy Satan and be done with wickedness?" Unfortunately, wickedness would not expire with the end of Satan, for his rebel spirit entered into the world in Eden and intruded into humanity (1 Jn. 2:16). Death and rebellion have been passed down to every generation since that time (Rom. 5:12). Summarizing the state of the human heart, the prophet Jeremiah wrote, *"The heart is deceitful above all things, and desperately wicked; who can know it? I, the Lord, search the heart, I test the mind, even to give every man according to his ways, according to the fruit of his doings"* (Jer. 17:9-10). Before destroying Satan, God will allow him to test the human heart's fortitude for godliness, and find it lacking. While enjoying God's fellowship in a perfect environment, both the first man (Adam) and the last humans on earth before it is destroyed (Rev. 20:11; 21:1; 1 Pet. 3:10) are shown to be incapable of pleasing God when tempted to sin against Him.

Man, left to himself, will always go his own way; he will turn away from God (Isa. 53:6). God provided a righteous solution for human rebellion by judging His Son Jesus Christ in our place and giving those who would trust in Him eternal life. Those who will not trust in God's means of salvation in Christ will experience eternal death in hell. So, no matter when individuals live, no matter what dispensation of accountability is present when they lived, all the redeemed (those justified by faith) will experience the first resurrection and enter into the Eternal State; all others will receive resurrected bodies before being cast into the Lake of Fire. These are the only two types of eternal resurrections that the Bible identifies – one to everlasting life and one to everlasting torment and separation from God.

The Second and Final Resurrection

Satan's final rebellion will end when the earth is destroyed at the conclusion of Christ's Millennial Kingdom. At that time, God will judge the wicked and cast them into the Lake of Fire. This spiritual abode is often referred to as "hell," and was originally created for the purpose of punishing Satan and his fallen angels (Matt. 25:41). Before God creates a new heaven and earth, He will resurrect those who would not receive the truth of salvation by faith. God is a good record-keeper and is faithful to uphold His Word. A number of books will be opened at this divine trial to demonstrate that God is fully cognizant of sin and just in punishing the wicked for their sins. In fact, the wicked, knowing their own guilt, will not attempt to plead their case before Him (Ps. 64:1; Rom. 3:19). Consequently, all who are tried at the Great White Throne Judgment are found guilty of violating God's perfect, righteous standard.

God's minimum requirement to enter into heaven is sinless perfection. Committing just one sin during one's entire life will prevent entrance into God's presence, that is, unless one has been declared righteous in Christ. Though the Christian is not sinless, he or she has a position of sinless perfection in Christ, and indeed, because of that union should sin less (Rom 6:1-4). As no one can undo one morally wrong act through the performance of many good ones, it is impossible to enter heaven by doing good works (Rom. 4:3-4; Eph. 2:8-9).

To believe that one is deserving of heaven through doing good deeds is an offensive notion to God, for that would mean that His judgment of His own Son on our behalf did not sufficiently satisfy His righteous demand for justice. This mindset means that individuals are really trusting in themselves and not in Christ alone for salvation. It is the erroneous message of world religion that you can improve your own spiritual essence or position through personal effort – essentially, you don't need a Savior. World religion says, "do, do, do," while biblical Christianity proclaims, "done, done, done." The former promotes personal effort for salvation, while the latter acknowledges that only personal faith in a Savior can save. Accordingly, everyone resurrected to stand before God at the Great White Throne judgment will be found guilty and cast into the Lake of Fire (Rev. 20:11-15).

Summary

With the understanding that the first resurrection occurs in stages and is unto everlasting life with the Lord, and the second resurrection is unto everlasting death in the Lake of Fire, let us investigate different views of their timing. In the next two chapters we will identify and investigate prevalent millennial and rapture views held by the Church from the whole of Scripture. We begin with Millennial Views.

Millennial Views

Some Christians believe that Christ's millennial reign is occurring now in a spiritual sense and that there will be no literal earthly kingdom where Christ restores Israel and rules on the throne of David for a thousand years. Others believe that the spiritual blessings of the Kingdom Age will be realized during the millennial reign of Christ. What is evident in either case is that the masses of humanity will not be anticipating the Lord's return to the earth to judge wickedness. In fact, Scripture states that they will be completely surprised by the Lord's Second Coming to the earth.

Three days before Christ's crucifixion, His disciples asked Him, *"What will be the sign of Your coming, and of the end of the age?"* (Matt. 24:3). The Lord responded to their question by describing several escalating signs of the coming Tribulation Period and detailing chronologically events that will occur during those seven years. The Lord concluded by giving the following warning:

> *But of that day and hour knows no man ... but as the days of Noah were so shall also the coming of the Son of Man be. For as in the days that were before the flood they were eating and drinking, marrying and giving in marriage, until the day that Noah entered into the ark. And knew not until the flood came, and took them all away, so shall also the coming of the Son of Man be* (Matt. 24:36-39).

The days prior to the Lord's Second Coming will be similar to the behavior of man in Noah's day. Sexual perversion and unceasing wickedness will characterize the days just prior to judgment. Man will be living for all the pleasure life can offer and have no remorse for the Creator's grieving heart. Noah's contemporaries lived like they had flood insurance, but the only insurance was the ark. Likewise today, in our post-Christian society, man lives for the day, not realizing that judgment is coming and that the good news of Jesus Christ is the only means of escape.

When will the Lord's Second Advent occur in relationship to the establishment of His kingdom? There are several viewpoints held by the Church and various cults, and space does not allow scrutiny of every view. The following five primary millennial views will be evaluated:

Amillennialism – Good (the kingdom of God) and evil continue to grow in the world until Christ returns to the earth to defeat evil once and for all, thus beginning the eternal state. This view spiritualizes Christ's kingdom (i.e., there is no literal millennial reign of Christ on earth).

Postmillennialism – Believers are diligently working to usher in Christ's kingdom on earth through gospel outreach efforts. Once properly prepared, Christ will return to the earth; this event will be the culmination of the kingdom.

Preterism – A literal-historical view that considers all major prophetic events to have been fulfilled in the first century. Hence, there is no rapture of the Church, no Tribulation Period, and no Millennial Kingdom to come. Some moderate Preterists believe in a literal second coming of Christ to the earth to establish a state of eternal bliss.

Adventism – In 1844, Christ entered the final stage of atoning ministry to judge and cleanse the redeemed in preparation of His second coming when saints will be taken to heaven for 1000 years and wickedness infests the world. All is destroyed at the end of the millennium.

Premillennialism – Christ will return to the earth at the end of the Tribulation Period to establish His righteous kingdom and reign on the earth for one thousand years.

Amillennial View

AMILLENNIAL VIEW

Between His two advents, Christ rules over a spiritual kingdom in the hearts of believers.

↑ **Spiritual Kingdom** ↓

Resurrection   2nd Advent

The Kingdom Age
Non-literal earthly kingdom

Framework

Covenant Theology views the Abrahamic covenant as conditional in nature. Some aspects were fulfilled but what the Jews failed to receive has been transferred to the Church (the Israel of today). Accordingly, the kingdom that Christ spoke of ruling, only exists in the hearts of believers and will continue in that domain until His Second Advent when He establishes a new heaven and earth. As no literal earthly kingdom is ever realized, Covenant Theology holds an Amillennial view.

Theological Support For

- Prophecy in the Bible demands a symbolic approach of interpretation (e.g. the millennial reign of Christ in Rev. 20:1-6 is spiritually occurring within the Church now).

- History is moving toward the goal of the total redemption and restoration of the Universe (Eph. 1:10; Col. 1:18).
- The New Testament sometimes equates Israel and the Church as one (Acts 13:32-39; Gal. 6:15; 1 Pet. 2:9).
- The conditional nature of Old Testament covenants indicates that fulfillment of these, or the lack of fulfillment, is transferred to the Church through Jesus Christ (Gal. 3:16).
- The millennium is figurative and presently occurring in that it includes the entire period commencing with Christ's enthronement at the right hand of the Father (Acts 2:29-33) and continues until His Second Advent.

Biblical Arguments Against

- The Abrahamic covenant was unconditional and to the nation of Israel, but has "spill over" blessings to all nations (Rom. 4:16-17; 11:16-22).
- Psalm 89:30-37 specifically addresses the results of a faithless Israel. Rather than Israel being permanently replaced, God uses this circumstance to repeatedly confirm His promises to never abandon Israel.
- Inconsistent hermeneutics; much spiritualization of Scripture is required to ensure that the framework holds together (e.g. a literal kingdom age on the earth will exist per Revelation 20-21). The fact that all the prophecies concerning Christ's first advent were fulfilled literally supplies the divine hermeneutic for interpreting the prophecies pertaining to His Second Coming.
- No "covenant of grace" is specifically mentioned in Scripture (a coined term to support view).
- The spiritual reality of the "kingdom of God" began with Christ; it has not always been. The view sees no need for a future kingdom: Christ's return is equated with the eternal state.
- The New Covenant was established with Judah and Israel, not Gentiles (Heb. 8:8; Isa. 45:17-19; Jer. 31:31-34).
- Christ has not yet received His kingdom, whose throne must be in Jerusalem (Isa. 66:10-21; Zech. 8:20-23); He presently sits at the right hand of His Father and on His Father's throne (Rev. 3:21). His throne will be in and over Israel (2 Sam. 7:8-16).

OT Scripture Describing Christ's Future Kingdom on Earth

- Zechariah 14: The nations gathered against Jerusalem and the city is conquered. The Lord returns to the earth (splits the Mount of Olives). The nations opposing Israel are destroyed and Jerusalem becomes the religious center of the World. If nations do not come to Jerusalem to worship, then they are swiftly judged. This is clearly not the eternal state, nor have these events occurred yet.
- Isaiah 11: Describes the Millennial Kingdom under Christ: children play with poisonous snakes, lions eat grass, wolves dwell with lambs, and the whole earth is full of the glory of God. Obviously, these conditions do not characterize the natural order today. Note: Isaiah speaks of the existence of seas during the Kingdom Age, but there are no seas in the New Earth (Rev. 21:2).
- Ezekiel 36-39: Christ will gather all Jews dwelling in the nations back to Israel. The Jewish nation will receive a clean heart and the indwelling Holy Spirit so that they can worship their Messiah in Jerusalem. These events are yet future.
- Ezekiel 40: The millennial temple described by Ezekiel has specific dimensions and is to be erected in Jerusalem. It has not been built yet.

Birth Announcements Declaring God's Intentions for Israel

- Gabriel to Mary (Luke 1:32-33): Jesus shall inherit the throne of David and reign over the twelve tribes of Israel forever.
- Mary to Elizabeth (Luke 1:55): Christ to bring about the complete fulfillment of the Abrahamic covenant.
- Statements of Zechariah (Luke 1:67-80): Christ to deliver Israel from their enemies (v. 71) and to fulfill the Abrahamic covenant (vv. 72-73). Israel will serve the Messiah in holiness and righteousness (vv. 74-75).
- Statements of Simeon (Luke 2:25-35): Christ to be a revelation to the Gentiles and the glory of Israel (v. 32).

Conclusion

The Abrahamic covenant is not complete – Christ's coming to establish His kingdom is yet future.

- The Abrahamic covenant consisted of building a nation, occupying a land, and that all nations of the world would be blessed through Abraham (speaking of the Messiah).
- Israel does not occupy the land that God allotted to them yet (Gen 15:18).
- Israel is not in the land specified and the millennial tribal allotments have not been delegated yet (Ezek. 47:13-23).

Postmillennial View

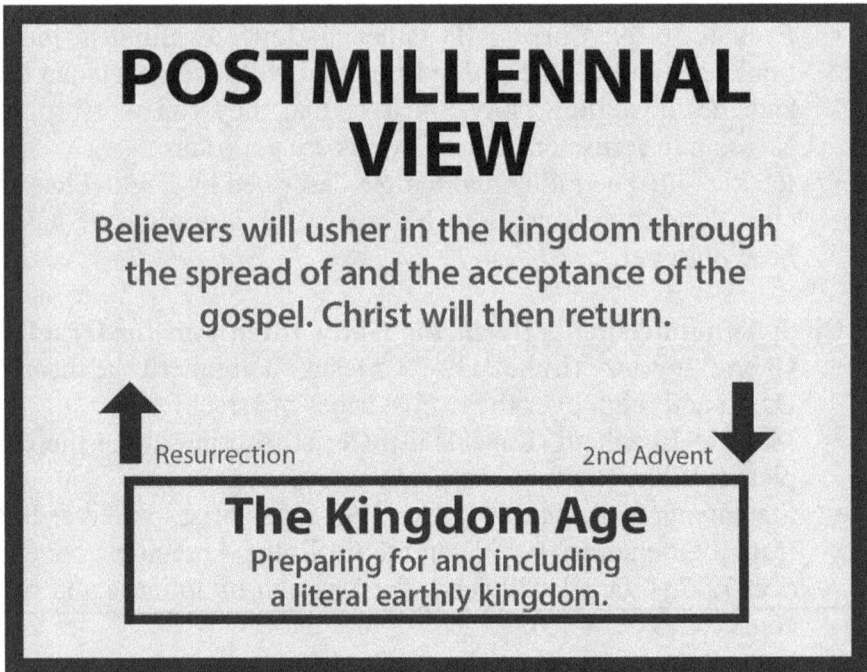

POSTMILLENNIAL VIEW

Believers will usher in the kingdom through the spread of and the acceptance of the gospel. Christ will then return.

Resurrection   2nd Advent

The Kingdom Age
Preparing for and including a literal earthly kingdom.

Framework

Proponents of this view believe that the kingdom of God was established on earth with Christ's first advent. Specifically, it started with His resurrection and will conclude with His second coming to the earth. This kingdom is now being expanded through the teaching and preaching of God's Word, especially through gospel outreach efforts, such as the work of missionaries in remote places. Once the entire world is Christianized, a long period of peace and prosperity will occur. This era is spoken of as the Millennium and reaches its zenith with Christ's return to the earth to usher in the eternal state. In effect, those holding this view are working to usher in the Kingdom without the King.

Theological Support For

- The universal preaching of the Gospel throughout the earth is promised by Christ (Matt. 28:18-20).
- Salvation will come to all nations, tribes, peoples, and tongues (Rev. 7:9-10).
- Much evidence indicates that wherever the gospel has been preached in the world, social and moral conditions improve.
- The ruling of the Holy Spirit within a believer's heart is, in a spiritual sense, a millennium (John 14-15).

Biblical Arguments Against

- The Great Commission does not promise universal gospel proclamation. The disciples were commanded to preach the gospel among the nations and disciple those who responded to it. This would continue until the Lord's return to gather up His Church, thus marking the end of the Church Age, not Christ's kingdom.
- While there will be representatives from every nation, tribe, people, and tongue in heaven, there is no universal promise that the masses will turn to Christ or even that most will be saved. In fact, the Lord Jesus stated that the opposite was true – most would not repent, but rather remain on the wide road leading to destruction (Matt. 7:13-14).
- The great evangelistic efforts of the nineteenth and twentieth centuries brought the gospel to many parts of the world, yet, sadly, the spiritual condition of humanity is in decline. This is

consistent with what Scripture states will happen prior to the Lord's return (Matt. 24:3-14; 1 Tim. 4:1-5; 2 Tim. 3:1-7).

• Revelation 20 refers to many specific events that occur during a specific one-thousand year period of time, which is referred to six times in the chapter. The millennial rule of Christ is not merely the Holy Spirit's influence within the believer's heart; it is Christ exalted and honored by all those dwelling on the earth.

Conclusion

In many respects, postmillennialism is really only an optimistic form of amillennialism; therefore the same conclusion is warranted. The only fundamental difference between these theological frameworks is that postmillennialism believes most of the world will be converted to Christ, whereas amillennialism does not. Neither viewpoint allows for a literal one-thousand year reign of Christ. In fact, the millennium is spiritual in substance and its length is undefined. Most postmillennial proponents permit a brief apostasy or resurgence of evil just prior to Christ's advent to judge evil once and for all.

Preterism

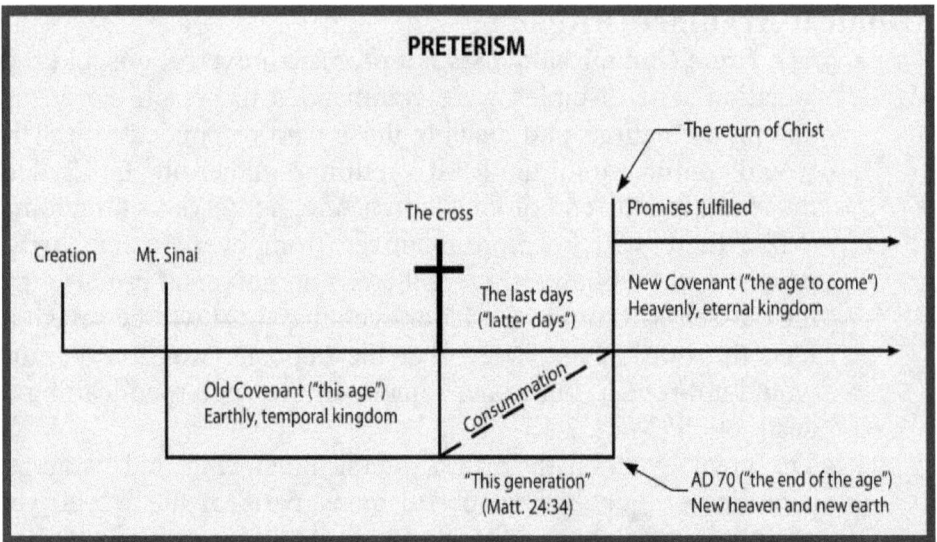

PRETERISM

The return of Christ

The cross

Creation   Mt. Sinai

Promises fulfilled

The last days ("latter days")

New Covenant ("the age to come") Heavenly, eternal kingdom

Old Covenant ("this age") Earthly, temporal kingdom

Consummation

"This generation" (Matt. 24:34)

AD 70 ("the end of the age") New heaven and new earth

Definition

The term *Preterit* is the Latin word for "past." Preterists believe that all the major events of Bible prophecy have already occurred. Consequently, there is no future rapture of the Church, literal seven-year Tribulation Period, literal Antichrist, conversion of Israel, battle of Armageddon, nor one-thousand year reign of Christ.

History

The view was developed in the late sixteenth century by Jesuit friar Luis de Alcazar to defend the Catholic Church against the attack of Protestant reformers. He interpreted Revelation 4-11 as the Church's conflict with Judaism until the destruction of Jerusalem in AD 70. The Church's struggle against paganism, which ended with the fall of Rome in AD 476, was said to be consistent with Revelation 12-19. Alcazar taught that the remaining portion of Revelation represented the glories of papal Rome. This historical interpretation affirmed that nearly all prophecies in the book of Revelation and the Olivet Discourse (Matt. 24-25) had already been fulfilled in the five centuries of church history. Thus, the harlot and the apostasy spoken of in Revelation 17 were not associated with the Roman Catholic Church because this prophecy had already been fulfilled during the Roman Empire.

Framework

A more aggressive form of Preterism has gained popularity in recent years and is now the most widely-held version of this historical-interpretive approach. Modern Preterism states that all the prophecies contained in the book of Revelation were fulfilled prior to the destruction of Jerusalem in AD 70. Accordingly, the Tribulation Period was the fall of Israel and the great apostasy of the Church supposedly occurred during the apostolic era. Moderate preterists do anticipate the resurrection of believers at the Second Advent of Christ to the earth and are thus, generally speaking, postmillennial in their thinking (i.e., they are preparing the kingdom for Christ's return). Most preterists would believe the following to be true:

- Nero was the Antichrist. There will be no future individual Antichrist.

129

- The Tribulation Period is over; it occurred when Rome besieged Jerusalem in AD 66-70.
- Christ "returned" in the clouds in AD 70 to witness the destruction of Jerusalem by the Roman army.
- God replaced Old Testament Israel with the Church.
- Armageddon already happened in AD 70 (e.g. the fall of "Babylon" in Rev. 18 refers to the destruction of Jerusalem by the Romans).
- Satan is already bound in the abyss and cannot hinder the spread of the Gospel (i.e., Rev. 20 has already been fulfilled).
- We are already in the Millennium, but it is not literal. Some preterists equate the entire Church Age with the Millennium.

Theological Support For
- Revelation 1:1: Christ told His disciples that He would come *"quickly."*
- Matthew 24:34: Christ said, *"This generation shall not pass away"* without seeing the Lord's coming.
- Matthew 16:28: *"Some standing here, which shall not taste of death, till they see the Son of Man coming in His kingdom."*

Biblical Support Against
Specific Considerations
- The imminent, not necessarily the immediate, return of Christ was anticipated by the disciples:
  - John (AD 90): *"It is the last times"* (1 Jn. 2:18). *"He shall appear that we may have confidence and not be ashamed before Him at His coming"* (1 Jn. 2:28).
  - Paul (AD 60): *"Then we who are alive and remain shall be caught up with Him"* (1 Thess. 4:17). *"We look for the Savior, the Lord Jesus, who shall change our lowly body, that it may be fashioned like His glorious body"* (Phil. 3:20-21). *"We shall not all sleep, but we shall all be changed"* (1 Cor. 15:51).
  - James (AD 45): *"The coming of the Lord draws near"* (Jas. 5:8).

- Peter (AD 66): *"That you be looking for the coming day of the Lord"* (2 Pet. 3:10-14). *"Christ's coming is at hand"* (2 Pet. 4:7).
- In Matthew 24:34, the word "generation" must be interpreted with the phrase "all these things." All the things described in Matthew 24 have not occurred yet – thus this cannot be a past generation of people.
- Matthew 16:28 reads: *"Some standing here, which shall not taste of death, till they see the Son of Man coming in His kingdom."* Peter confirmed the meaning of the Lord's statement: some of the disciples saw the transfiguration of Christ, the glory of His kingdom, shortly afterwards (2 Pet. 1:16-18).
- Preterism interprets virtually all of Revelation and Old Testament prophecies concerning the Day of the Lord in a way that mostly nullifies their literal meaning.
- Preterism negates the Lord's commands to watch and be ready for His coming. If the Lord has already come for the Church and rewarded her, what hope is there for believers to live for Christ today?

The Date of Revelation

Preterism places the book of Revelation prior to Nero's death in AD 68, but nearly all biblical scholars agree with a date of AD 95 for Revelation. Mark Hitchcock explains: "While Preterism has many weaknesses, the Achilles' heel of this view is the early date the proponents assign to the book of Revelation. The external evidence for a late date of Revelation (AD 95) is overwhelming."[1]

Was Nero the Antichrist?

- Nero did not stand up in the temple at Jerusalem and proclaim himself to be God (2 Thess. 2:4).
- Nero did not slaughter a large portion of the world population for not taking his mark (Rev. 13:15).
- Nero did not rule over every tribe and nation as the Antichrist will (Rev. 13:7).
- Nero did not have a high-profile prophet who performs spectacular miracles; the Antichrist will (Rev. 13:13).

• Christ did not return visibly to put Nero to death, nor was his death 1260 days after the abomination of desolation, which also did not occur in Nero's day.

Conclusion

Amillennialism fails to apply a literal interpretation of Scripture concerning future things. Preterism attempts to correct this but its historical reckoning of first century events does not fit the cataclysmic worldwide situation described in the book of Revelation. Consequently, Nero was not the Antichrist, the battle of Armageddon did not occur, and the Church is still on the earth awaiting Christ's coming. Preterism therefore results in two major ills: First, it promotes anti-Semitism in the name of Jesus Christ. Second, Peter warns *"that scoffers will come in the last days, walking according to their own lusts, and saying, 'Where is the promise of His coming?'"* (2 Pet. 3:3-4). Preterism denies believers of their blessed hope – the promised coming of the Lord Jesus Christ for His Church!

Adventism

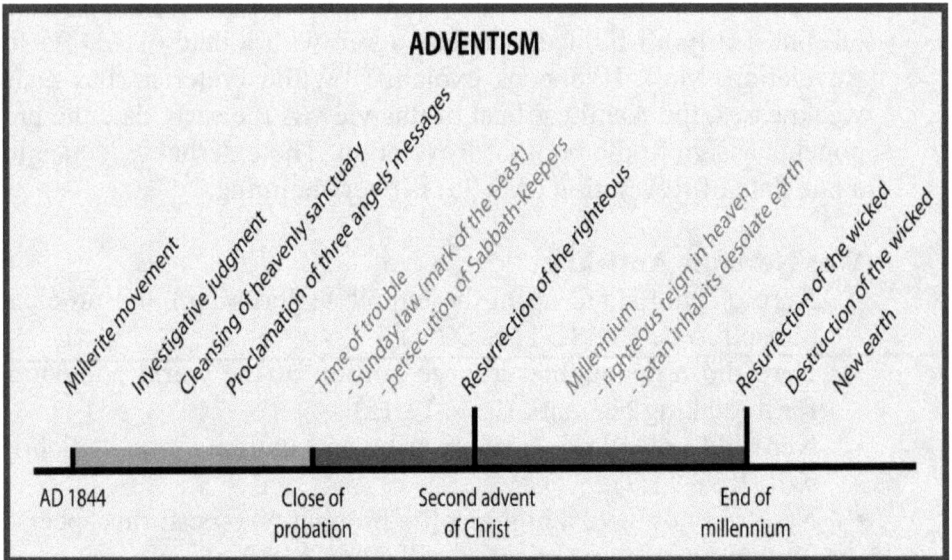

132

Concerning Israel, Adventism holds a similar view of Israel to both Amillennialism and Preterism – God is done with the Jewish nation. Much of Adventism today is governed by the writings of Ellen White in the mid-nineteenth century. In her book *The Great Controversy* published in 1858, she states:

> Satan rejoiced that the Jews were safe in his snare. They still continued their useless forms, their sacrifices and ordinances. ... The long-suffering of God toward Jerusalem, only confirmed the Jews in their stubborn impenitence. In their hatred and cruelty toward the disciples of Jesus, they rejected the last offer of mercy. Then God withdrew His protection from them, and removed His restraining power from Satan and his angels, and the nation was left to the control of the leader she had chosen.[1]

Because the Jewish nation rejected Christ, Adventism teaches that God has abandoned them forever. They are under Satan's control and destined to be destroyed.

Framework

The framework of Adventism is complex; it suffices here to summarize some of its key tenets, which are said to have theological support.

The Second Coming of Christ

The eschatological teachings of Seventh-day Adventism are quite complex, especially in reference to events which supposedly have or will occur in heaven prior to Christ's Second Coming. Adventists do believe that the Second Coming of Christ to the earth will be sudden, literal, visible, and personal. There will be no battle of Armageddon at that time, as Adventist spiritualize the Revelation 14 reference to this event and understand it to be speaking of a world-wide spiritual battle for the minds of men prior to Christ's coming. At the time of the Lord's coming, the righteous will experience resurrection and be translated to be with Christ, who returns to heaven. Thus, they believe in a Post-Tribulation rapture of the Church. Adventism does not believe that the souls of the righteous are in heaven presently, but are rather asleep in their graves until the day of their resurrection.

133

The Kingdom Age

The Second Coming of the Lord Jesus to resurrect the righteous from the earth marks the initiation of the Millennium, a time in which Christ will reign in heaven for one thousand years with those who experience the first resurrection. Christ also judges the rest of mankind on earth (i.e., the wicked) at His Second Coming. This leaves the earth devoid of human life so that Satan and his angels can occupy it during the Millennium. Adventists see this as the binding of Satan in the bottomless pit spoken of in Revelation 20:1. However, Scripture states that after one thousand years, he will be loosed from this abode to again roam the earth to deceive the nations before finally being thrown into the Lake of Fire (Rev. 20:7-10). Thus, it is clear that earth is not the bottomless pit and that there are still many living on the earth at the time of his release.

Destruction of the earth

At the conclusion of the Millennium, Adventists believe that Christ will again return to earth together with the righteous and the New Jerusalem, the Holy City coming down from heaven (Rev. 21:10). Christ will then judge all the wicked, including Satan and his angels, who surround this city. At this point, all the wicked will experience the "second resurrection," and suffer immediate annihilation in the Lake of Fire. This is the second death (Rev. 20:8). Adventists do not believe that hell is a literal state/place where individuals consciously suffer eternal punishment. After judging all the wicked, God will create a new earth where the redeemed will enjoy eternal life free of the filth of sin and the suffering it caused.

Theological Support For

As summarized above.

Biblical Support Against

The Antichrist and 200 million who gather with him in Israel to fight against the Lord will engage in a literal battle called the battle of Armageddon (Rev. 9:16; 16:16). Christ will return from heaven to defeat this army (Rev. 19) and a detailed, literal account of their destruction is provided in Zechariah 14. The slaughter is so extensive that the blood from those slain gushes out of the battlefield for some 182 miles (Rev. 14:19-20).

Contrary to the Adventism teachings, Paul declares that immediately upon death, the souls of believers go to heaven to be with the Lord prior to their bodily resurrection (2 Cor. 5:8; Phil. 1:23). John confirms the same truth of those believers who die during the Tribulation Period (Rev. 6:9-11; 20:4). Furthermore, the Lord Jesus described the place of torment, Hades, that the wicked consciously reside in prior to their resurrection for final judgment (Luke 16:19-31). This judgment occurs after the Kingdom Age and after all the wicked souls in Hades have experienced resurrection to stand before Christ at the Great White Throne (Rev. 20:11-15). All these individuals are condemned and thrown into the Lake of Fire where they *"shall be tormented day and night forever and ever"* (Rev. 20:10).

The Bible vividly describes the ultimate fate of those who reject God's truth. The following are terms used in association with Lake of Fire (hell):

- *"Shame and everlasting contempt"* (Dan. 12:2)
- *"Everlasting punishment"* (Matt. 25:46)
- *"Weeping and gnashing of teeth"* (Matt. 24:51)
- *"Unquenchable fire"* (Luke 3:17)
- *"Indignation and wrath, tribulation and anguish"* (Rom. 2:8-9)
- *"Their worm does not die* [putrid, endless agony]*"* (Mark 9:44)
- *"Everlasting destruction"* (2 Thess. 1:9)
- *"Eternal fire ... the blackness of darkness forever"* (Jude 7, 13)
- *"The fire is not quenched"* (Mark 9:46)

Revelation 14:10-11 tells us of the final, eternal destiny of the sinner: *"He shall be tormented with fire and brimstone ... the smoke of their torment ascended up forever and ever: and they have no rest day or night."* The Bible's teaching of eternal punishment for unforgiven sinners offends people; consequently, many are watering down the truth, teaching that hell is a state of non-existence or quick annihilation. Misrepresenting the truth to avoid its consequence is never a good idea.

Conclusion

Adventism, like Amillennialism, fails to apply a literal interpretation of Scripture concerning many future events prophesied in the Bible. Much of their eschatological teachings have developed because of the failed prophecies of Ellen White and William Miller in the mid-nineteenth century. As Christ did not literally return to the earth October 22, 1844, as foretold, those following Miller's teachings split into various groups to explain the disappointment. One group postulated that Miller's assumption that the sanctuary to be cleansed was not the earth (Dan. 8:14), but the heavenly sanctuary. Why God's sanctuary in heaven would need cleansing is unknown. Thus, the missed date was not Christ's coming to the earth, but only a non-biblical heavenly event. This group later became known as the Seventh-day Adventist Church.

Premillennialism

PREMILLENNIAL VIEW

Christ will return to the earth before the millennial kingdom commences. The kingdom ends with the destruction of the earth, followed by a new heaven and a new earth.

2nd Advent

The Kingdom Age
A literal earthly kingdom
spanning 1,000 years.

Framework

Premillennialism applies a literal interpretation of Scripture which views the spiritual aspects of God's kingdom today within believers as leading to a literal, earthly, and political fulfillment at Christ's return to the earth. This will be followed by His one-thousand-year peaceful and righteous reign on earth. The spiritual blessings of Christ enjoyed by believers today will benefit all who inhabit the earth in a coming day.

- **Classical Premillennialism** holds to a Post-Tribulation rapture of the Church.
- **Dispensational Premillennialism** sees Christ's coming for the Church prior to the Tribulation Period and Christ's Second Advent at the end of the Tribulation.

Theological Support For

Characteristics of Christ's Kingdom vs. the Eternal State

Christ's kingdom on earth is clearly distinct from the perfect conditions that will exist in the new heaven and new earth, which is often referred to as "the Eternal State." The prophesied conditions of each situation ensures that they cannot exist at the same time: Millennial conditions exist after Christ's Second Advent to the earth and Eternal State conditions exist after this world is destroyed and a new heaven and earth are created (Rev. 21-22).

Biblical Support For

The following passages confirm that the millennial rule of Christ occurs during a literal earthly kingdom that is not merely spiritual in nature, nor is it the same as the Eternal State. For the following reasons, this necessitates Christ's return to the earth prior to the Kingdom Age:

1. During Christ's Kingdom, (the Millennium), Jerusalem will be the religious center of the world and Christ will reign from Jerusalem over all the nations. All the inhabitants of the world will regularly come to Jerusalem to worship and to learn from Christ and all the earth will witness His glory (Isa. 2:1-5; 60:20; 66:18-20). This

situation is obviously not the Eternal State, as sinful people are still living in the world. The nations still have the capacity to rebel against Christ and will, according to Revelation 20. It also cannot exist until after Christ comes again to the earth at the end of the Tribulation Period. Thus, Christ's Second Advent will precede the Millennial Kingdom.

2. The Jews who live through the Tribulation Period will become the refined remnant which is restored to God (Rom. 9:27; 11:7-14; 11:23-25). This was prophesied extensively in the Old Testament (e.g. Joel 2:25-29; Zech. 12:8-10; Ezek. 36:17-36). The New Covenant, which Christ sealed with His own blood, was instituted with the house of Israel and the house of Judah in order to enable the future restoration of the nation (Heb. 8:8). Israel will behold Christ's splendor, glory, fruitfulness, and beauty and will appreciate Him (Isa. 4:2-4). This has not yet happened; the Jewish nation hates Christ and will continue to do so until they see Him return at the end of the Tribulation Period. Then they will recognize Him as their Messiah (Zech. 12:10).

3. Isaiah describes conditions on the earth after Christ removes the curses placed upon it due to the fall of man. All the wicked will be judged, the wolf shall dwell with the lamb, the leopard with the kid, the calf with the lion; the lion shall eat straw, and the child shall play by the hole of the asp (Isa. 11:1-8). Isaiah then says, *"For the earth shall be full of the knowledge of the Lord, as the waters cover the sea"* (Isa. 11:9). Ezekiel (Ezek. 47:18), Joel (Joel 3:18), and Zechariah (Zech. 14:8) described similar happenings, as well as noting that there are seas on the earth at this time. Since we know that the new earth does not have any seas (Rev. 21:1), we therefore conclude that the setting for these events must be after Christ returns to the earth, but before the earth is destroyed one thousand years later (Rev. 21:5-11). Obviously, the curses placed on the earth because of human sin have not been lifted yet, meaning the Millennium is yet to come (Rom. 8:19-22).

4. During the millennial reign of Christ, the Lord will be the light of the earth; there will be no need for sun or moon; also, He will drive violence from the earth (Isa. 60:18-20). This has clearly not happened yet.

5. The Abrahamic covenant (Gen. 12:1-3) involved building a nation, occupying a land, and blessing all nations of the world through Abraham (accomplished through the Messiah). The land allotted to the Jewish nation is specified in Genesis 15:18. However, Israel has never wholly possessed that land, meaning that this part of the covenant has not been fulfilled. The prophet Ezekiel states that the covenant will be fulfilled after Christ returns to the earth to establish His kingdom. Ezekiel specifies the future land allotments to be given to each tribe (Ezek. 47:13-23). This prophecy has not been fulfilled yet and certainly cannot be if the earth is destroyed. The covenant promise will be realized after the nations of the world honor Christ's authority – this will happen during His kingdom rule.

6. The Jewish people have been hated for centuries, but during Christ's rule on earth, the Jewish people will be greatly honored and appreciated by the nations (Zech. 8:20-23). They will readily come to Jerusalem to worship the Lord. Again, this event cannot be fulfilled by any other view than a pre-millennial return of Christ to the earth.

7. Once the Jews are restored to God, they will be returned to the Promised Land and never be removed from it again by Gentile powers (Amos 9:14-15).

8. Ezekiel 40-43 provides much detail pertaining to the dimensions and construction of the millennial temple in Jerusalem. Clearly, this temple has never been erected and since Christ is worshipped in this temple during the Millennium, He must be present during the Kingdom Age.

9. Isaiah 2:1-5 and 66:10-18 confirm that Jerusalem will be the religious center of the World and Christ shall reign from that city in His kingdom. All the earth shall see God's glory at this time. However, Isaiah spoke of a new heaven and new earth after this, which means the earthly Jerusalem will be gone (Isa. 51:16; 65:17). Thus, the Millennial Kingdom and the Eternal State cannot be the same.

10. Zechariah 14:1-9: The Lord returns to the earth, splits the Mount of Olives, and destroys attacking Gentile armies led by the Antichrist; He then makes Jerusalem His capital and rules the world from there. Those nations who do not come there to annually worship Christ will be punished (Isa. 60:12; Zech. 14:16-21). John says that when the Lord returns, He will *"rule the nations with a rod of iron"* (Rev. 19:15). Obviously, the nations are still present on the earth during Christ's rule over them and they need to be policed. This cannot be the Eternal State as there are no people in the new heaven and new earth who can rebel against Christ's rule (Rev. 22:1-5).

11. The seas and oceans on earth today will still be present during the Kingdom Age (Isa. 11:9; Ezek. 47:18; Zech. 14:8), but there will not be any seas in the new earth (Rev. 21:1).

12. Geographic locations on earth today, such as Jerusalem, Egypt, and Lebanon will exist in the Millennial Kingdom (Isa. 60:13; Joel 3:18; Zech. 14:16-21), but obviously will not in the new earth. The new heaven and earth will not be created until after the Kingdom Age is concluded, Satan's last rebellion on earth is quelled (Rev. 20:7-10), and the planet that we presently live on is obliterated (Isa. 34:4; 2 Pet. 3:10; Rev. 20:11).

Conclusion

Satan and his angels will be bound in the bottomless pit during Christ's Millennial Kingdom. At that time, the curses levied on the earth after the fall of man will be lifted. Those surviving the Tribulation Period and who did not take the mark of the beast will be permitted to live on earth during the Kingdom Age. This means there will still be a significant population living on earth with the old flesh nature which is prone to sin. However, any rebellion against Christ will be quickly judged (Zech. 14:16-21; Rev. 19:15). All the unfulfilled promises of God to Abraham, David, and their descendants will be fulfilled during the Kingdom Age. God does not break His promises.

After Satan is loosed from his prison, he will again deceive the nations into rebelling against Christ (Rev. 20:7-9). The spiritually restored nation of Israel and the glorified saints from the Old Testament, the Church Age, and the Tribulation Period will be ruling and reigning with Christ in various capacities at this time (Heb. 11:39-40; 1 Jn. 3:2; Rev. 20:4). These saints are not capable of rebelling against the Lord. However, all rebels that align with Satan will be destroyed with the earth and the souls of the unfaithful dead are then resurrected to stand before God at His Great White Throne to be judged. After verbally acknowledging Christ as Lord and bowing the knee to Him, these will be cast into the Lake of Fire (Rom. 14:11; Phil. 2:10-11). After destroying sin, death, and the old earth, God will create a New Heaven and New Earth, which has no defilement in it (Rev. 20:14-21:2). Here redeemed man will enjoy unbroken fellowship with God in paradise forever. This communion with man was desired by God from the beginning and, to some degree, was enjoyed with Adam in the Garden of Eden before the fall of mankind.

The various millennial views pertain to Christ's earthly kingdom and His Second Advent. Many prophecies were given to the nation of Israel to alert them to a time of sorrow which would occur just prior to Christ's Second Advent. Though the Church will reign and rejoice with Christ during this time, the Church's hope relates to its rapture from the earth which occurs prior to the Kingdom Age. Most of Christendom would agree with this statement, but with varying viewpoints as to when the rapture of the Church actually occurs prior to the Kingdom Age. With the above millennial views in mind, let us turn our attention to evaluating various rapture views.

Rapture Views

While most Christians believe in a literal Second Coming of Christ to the earth to judge the wicked, there are varying views as to how the Church fits into the events leading up to Christ's Second Advent. Some believe that Christ has already come for the Church and believers living in the world today just go to be with the Lord when they die. Others believe that the Tribulation Period just prior to the Kingdom Age will be used to refine the Church, who will then be honored with Christ at His coming. There are those who believe that Christ will not return until the Church prepares the kingdom for Him. Others believe that the Church will be on earth during part or most of the Tribulation Period, but will be protected to some extent. Furthermore, some believe that Christ will gather up the Church from the earth before working to refine and restore the Jewish nation to Himself during the Tribulation Period.

In this chapter, we will review the primary Tribulation views as each relates to the Church (i.e., in reference to when the rapture of the Church occurs). Each view will then be scrutinized with Scripture to highlight its strengths and weakness. It is noted that a few Christians hold to a Partial Rapture view, a position that states that only those believers "watching and waiting" for the Lord's coming will be raptured at various times prior to and during the seven-year Tribulation Period (Matt. 24:40-51). Both the Lord and Paul confirm that Christ is coming for the Church in its entirety (John 14:1; 1 Cor. 12:13; 15:51-52). Consequently, this teaching will not be specifically evaluated, as arguments against its tenets would be contained within the Mid-Tribulation and Pre-Wrath discussions.

Post-Tribulation Rapture

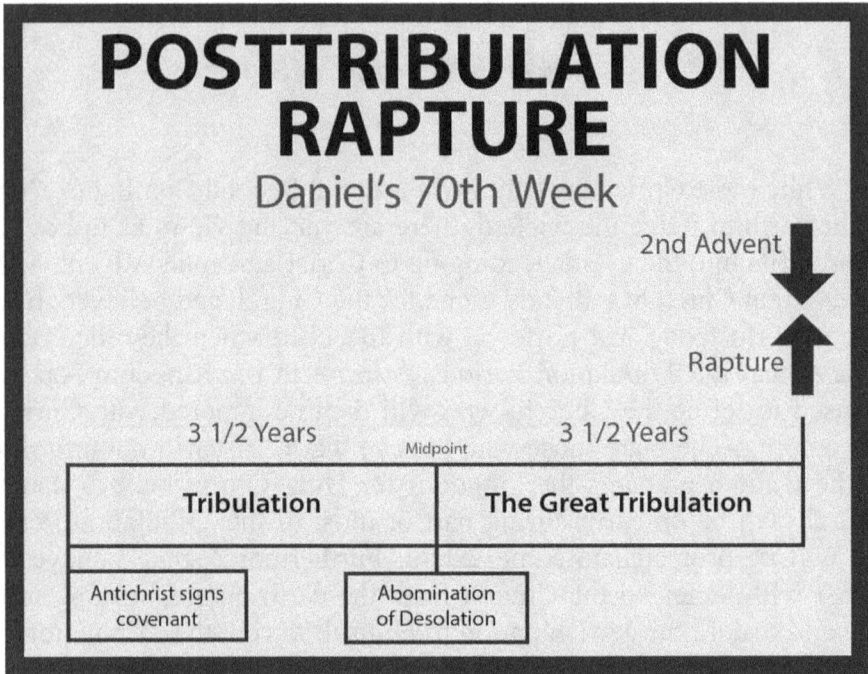

POSTTRIBULATION RAPTURE
Daniel's 70th Week

2nd Advent

Rapture

3 1/2 Years | Midpoint | 3 1/2 Years

Tribulation | The Great Tribulation

Antichrist signs covenant | Abomination of Desolation

- This position asserts that living believers will be raptured from the earth at Christ's Second Advent.
- The rapture is preceded by unmistakable signs (Matt. 24:3-31).
- The Church will be purified through the Tribulation Period, a view especially held by Roman Catholicism.
- The Church will be protected from Satan's wrath during the Tribulation Period (Rev. 3:10).

Arguments Against
- The Beast slaughters the Tribulation saints (Rev. 13:7). Though the Church has been persecuted through the centuries, it has not been overcome to this degree. Speaking of the Church, the Lord promised that the *"gates of hell would not prevail against it"* (Matt. 16:18). It is again noted that two-thirds of the Jews will

die during the Tribulation Period (Zech. 13:7-8). There is no promise to protect the Church during the Tribulation Period, only a remnant of Jews in a particular location (Rev. 12:12-17).

- The Church is seen coming with the Lord at the end of the Tribulation Period (Rev. 19:14); these saints are already wearing crowns on their heads, which were received earlier (Rev. 4). But how would that be possible since, according to this view, the Judgment Seat of Christ would have to occur after Christ's Second Coming to the earth? Clearly resurrected believers have already been rewarded prior to His Second Advent as these saints are wearing crowns when they depart heaven with the Lord.

- The scriptural distinction between "the day of Christ" and "the day of the Lord" is lost. The day of Christ refers to the rapture of the Church and the Judgment Seat of Christ where the value of the believer's work will be judged. Thus, the day of Christ is always spoken of in a positive light and is to be joyfully anticipated (1 Cor. 1:8; 5:5; 2 Cor. 1:14; Phil 1:6, 10; 2:16).

- Claiming that the 144,000 of Revelation 7 are the ones which populate the earth during the millennial reign of Christ negates the clear Jewish context of the passage (i.e., 12,000 Jews from each of the twelve tribes are identified).

- John admitted that he did not know who the saints were who had recently appeared with him in heaven. He was told by one of the elders that these were those who had been slaughtered by the Antichrist during the last half of the Tribulation (Rev. 7:14). Some believe that this great multitude is the Church which has been raptured from the world just before Christ's Second Advent. If that were the case, John would have certainly known some of these believers. These are the souls of Tribulation saints only, all of which will experience resurrection at Christ's Second Advent (Rev. 20:4).

145

- The shepherding trilogy of Psalm 22, 23, and 24 foretells the future work of the Lord Jesus in relationship to those He would save. In Psalm 22, the Lord is presented as the "Good Shepherd" who lays His life down for the sheep at Mount Calvary (John 10:9-11). In Psalm 23, the present sanctifying work of the Lord Jesus leading is pictured – He is faithfully leading His sheep through the valley of shadows and providing for all their needs. The writer of Hebrews highlights this ongoing ministry of the Lord Jesus who is proclaimed to be the "Great Shepherd" (Heb. 13:20-21). Finally, Psalm 24 speaks of the Lord gathering up His people to Mount Zion, heaven. This shepherding ministry of Christ is acknowledged by Peter; He is the "Chief Shepherd" who will return and gather His sheep to Himself (1 Pet. 5:4). This is speaking of the return of Christ to the air to "snatch away" from the earth those who have truly believed on Him.

  Psalm 24 notes two entrances of the resurrected Lord Jesus into heaven. The first entrance was as a victor after His resurrection. At Calvary, Christ triumphed over Satan, the prince of the world (Ps. 24:8; John 12:31-32). He entered heaven alone at this time and sat down at the right hand of majesty on high (Heb. 1:3; Rev. 3:21). Later He leaves this privileged position to return to the earth to gather up His saints (Ps. 24:9). Thus, at His second entrance into heaven He will not be alone; He is the King of Glory – the Lord of hosts (Ps. 24:10). This shepherding trilogy from Psalms shows that resurrected saints return to heaven with Christ and are not raptured at the end of the Tribulation Period to just be with Him on the earth.

- Paul confirms that Christians will be presented blameless before God in glory (i.e., in heaven) at the appearing of the Lord Jesus Christ to remove them from the earth (Col. 3:4; 1 Thess. 3:13).

Conclusion

The Lord only promises to protect a remnant of Jews during the Tribulation Period and they will be kept safe at a specific location in the wilderness (Rev. 12:13-17). Other believers are slaughtered by the

Antichrist at this time (Dan. 7:21; Rev. 13:7). Given the twenty-one plagues recorded in Revelation 6 through 16, most of the world population will die during the Tribulation Period. For example, one-fourth of all mankind dies in the fourth seal judgment by war, famine and pestilence (Rev. 6:8) and one-third of mankind perishes by fire in the sixth trump judgment (Rev. 16:18). If the Lord waited until the end of the Tribulation Period to rapture His Church from the world, there would be few if any believers to rescue.

Pre-Wrath Rapture View

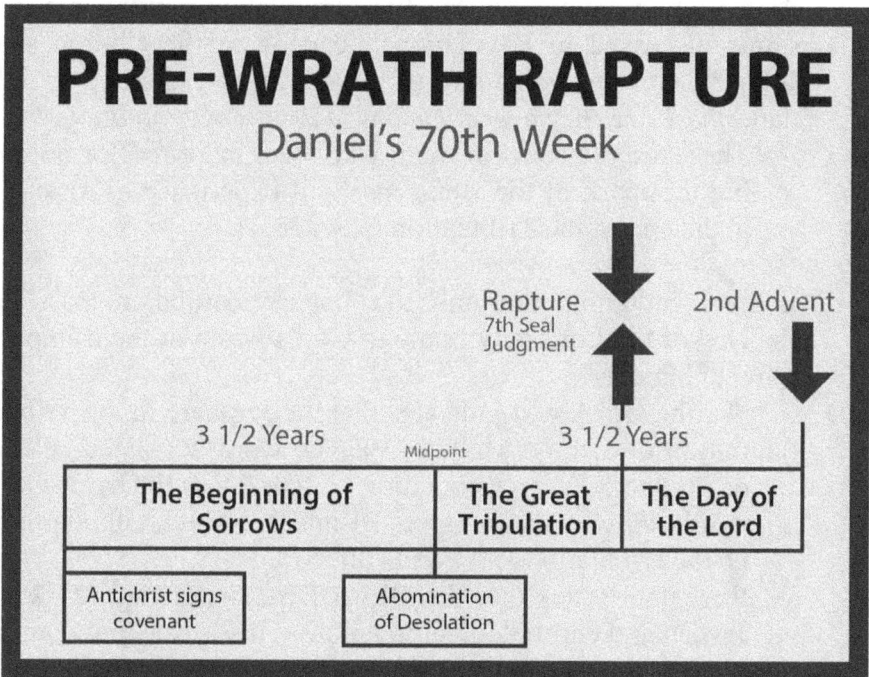

PRE-WRATH RAPTURE
Daniel's 70th Week

Rapture
7th Seal
Judgment

2nd Advent

3 1/2 Years   Midpoint   3 1/2 Years

| The Beginning of Sorrows | The Great Tribulation | The Day of the Lord |

Antichrist signs covenant

Abomination of Desolation

- Marvin Rosenthal first presented this view in his book *The Pre-wrath Rapture of the Church* (1990).
- He teaches that the Lord will take the Church to heaven between the sixth and the seventh Seal judgments, and then the Day of the Lord will begin.

- He views those in Revelation 7 as the Church who were raptured in order to escape God's judgment on earth.
- He states that the Great Tribulation is a period between the Abomination of Desolation and the Day of the Lord (i.e., it includes the first six seal judgments). The Day of the Lord is taught to be the trump and bowl judgments. The bowl judgments supposedly occur in the last 30 days before the doom of the Antichrist.
- He sees no difference between the day of Christ and the day of the Lord.

Arguments Against:

- As already mentioned in the Post-Tribulation rapture view, the saints discussed in Revelation 7 cannot be the Church since John did not recognize any of them. It was explained to John that *"these are they who come out of the great tribulation."*
  - These are the souls of them who were martyred for not taking the mark of the Beast and will experience glorification at the end of the Tribulation (Rev. 20:4).

- Is the Great Tribulation only the first six seal judgments? Does the Day of the Lord only relate to God's wrath in the trump and bowl judgments?
  - No, the Greek text indicates that the Jews are in the Tribulation prior to this (Matt. 24:9). The word translated "afflicted" in the KJV or "tribulation" in the RV is the same Greek word *thlipsis* used in verses 21 and 29, which talk about the Great Tribulation and events afterwards.
  - Rosenthal states that the Olivet Discourse (Matt. 24-25) is Jewish and chronological in nature. This is true, but contrary to his position, the Greek word usage referring to the Tribulation Period in Matthew 24 indicates that the Jews are in tribulation before and after the Abomination of Desolation. The elect refers to the Jews, but Rosenthal includes the Church within the reference (though he states this portion of Scripture pertains to the Jews).

- The Abomination of Desolation clearly occurs in the middle of the Tribulation Period (Dan. 9:27). The last half of the Tribulation Period, referred to as the Great Tribulation, begins with the Abomination of Desolation (Matt. 24:15) and ends with the destruction of Antichrist (Dan. 12).
  - The desolation occurs just after the seventh trump judgment and is exactly 1260 days (Rev. 12:6) or 42 months (Rev. 13:5) or *"a time, times, and half a time"* (Dan. 12:7; Rev. 12:14) before Christ's return to destroy the Beast.

- Since Daniel's seventieth week (Dan. 9:27) is associated with a seven-year period in which the Antichrist will rule the world (this period begins with a peace treaty with Israel), the time of tribulation in Matthew 24 must be one and the same with Daniel's seventieth week (the time of Jacob's trouble; Jer. 30:7).

- The scriptural distinction between the day of Christ (i.e., the Rapture of the Church) and the day of the Lord (i.e., God intervenes on earth to judge) is lost. Some passages referring to these days must be heavily spiritualized to make the pre-wrath view fit.
  - For example, Rosenthal states that the destruction of the earth with fervent heat and the creation of a new earth cannot be taken literally (2 Pet. 3:10-13). Peter refers to this as the day of the Lord. Rosenthal teaches, as many cults do, that Christ just purifies the existing earth.

- Rosenthal's position that the Church is saved from God's wrath but not the human and natural disasters associated with pre-trumpet judgments is not supported by Revelation 3:10. (Much of humanity dies prior to the trump judgments.)

- Some suggest that the Church will be delivered from wrath during the Tribulation Period, as Israel was delivered from the plagues in Egypt, not by being physically removed but by being supernaturally preserved. Yet the promise of Revelation 3:10 is that the Church will be kept from (Greek preposition "ek," which means "out of") not only the trial of that hour, but from the "hour of trial" itself.

— If "kept out" somehow means "kept in," why then are the Tribulation saints not kept from hardship; many are slaughtered for their testimony (Rev. 6:10-11; Matt. 24:22)!

Conclusion

The Pre-wrath view spiritualizes several key passages pertaining to future events. There is a dispensational confusion of the Olivet Discourse (Matt. 24-25): it cannot be Jewish in nature (i.e., God's working to restore the Jewish nation) and also pertain to the Church Age. There is no promise to protect the Church during the Tribulation Period; there is, however, a promise that a remnant from the twelve tribes of Israel will be protected from the Antichrist. Christ is the One breaking the seals of the scroll in heaven which is unleashing judgments on earth. He is thus solely responsible for these judgments. Consequently, to say that the seal judgments are not the wrath of God would be ludicrous.

Mid-Tribulation Rapture View

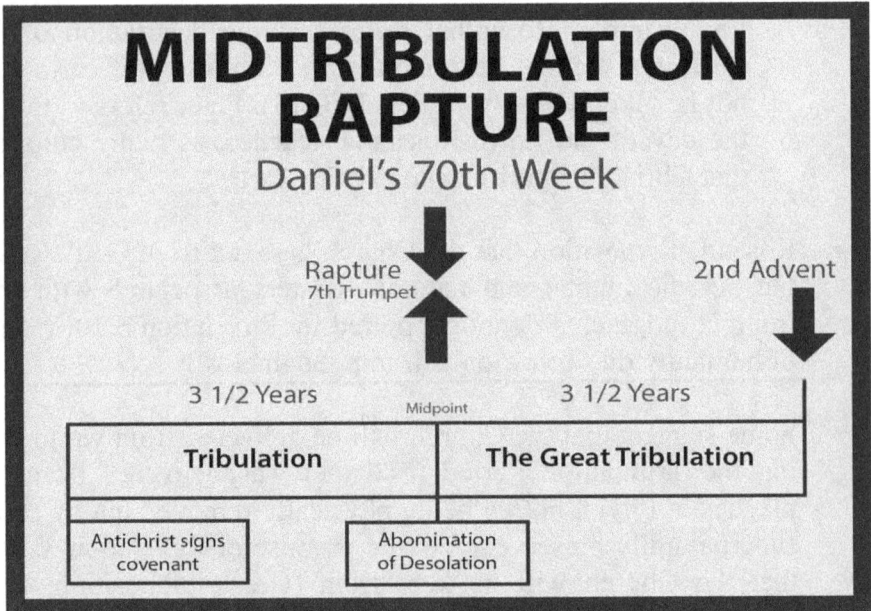

This view states that the Church will be taken up after the 7th trump judgment (Rev. 11) which supposedly occurs at the midpoint in the Tribulation Period (i.e., before the population on earth experiences severe loss of life). The timing is based on the terminology in Revelation 12. As in the Pre-Wrath Rapture view, this position does provide a distinction between the temporal events of the rapture of the Church (mid-tribulation) and the revelation of Christ (post-tribulation). The nation of Israel is restored at the latter event.

Arguments Against

- This view connects the last trump of 1 Corinthians 15:51-52 with the last trumpet judgment in Revelation. However, the seventh trumpet judgment of Revelation 8-11 is not the last trumpet blast to be heard during the Tribulation Period; there is another trump at the end of the Tribulation Period which is used to re-gather all Jews back to Israel (Matt. 24:31).
  - Jehovah used silver trumpets to call an assembly of His people together while they were wandering in the wilderness. In Exodus 19, a long blast of a trumpet, perhaps of a ram's horn, was used to signal the Israelites to gather at the base of Mount Sinai to meet the Lord. The mount quaked exceedingly, it burned like an overheated furnace, and thick billows of smoke ascended up from it into heaven. From the thick darkness, a deafening voice which increased in volume uttered words as if blasted from a trumpet. The people feared and were in awe of the Lord. This will be Israel's response when they are called to and restored to Jehovah at the end of the Tribulation Period.

- A majority of the world's population would already be dead by the seventh trumpet judgment, meaning that the Church would have suffered greatly if still on earth. Thus, the Mid-Tribulation Rapture view is similar to the Pre-Wrath mentality.
  - Example: one-fourth of mankind dies by famine, pestilence, war (Rev. 6:8), and a third of mankind dies by fire (Rev. 9:18).

- The emphasis of the midpoint of the Tribulation is on the abomination of desolation, not the rapture of the Church. The Antichrist will stop the Jewish sacrifices and proclaim himself to be God, thus breaking his covenant with Israel. The Antichrist then will try to annihilate every Jew on the planet and put to death those who will not take his mark (Rev. 12:14-17; 13:14-18).

- Paul states that two events will usher in the day of the Lord: the apostasy of the professing Church and the revealing of the man of sin, the Antichrist. The day of Christ, which refers to the rapture of the Church, precedes the day of the Lord, but the Mid-Tribulation Rapture view places the rapture of the Church in the day of the Lord. Paul wrote to ensure that the believers at Thessalonica understood this distinction and to confirm that they were not in the day of the Lord (2 Thess. 2:1-4).

- The Antichrist is not revealed until He who restrains sin (the Holy Spirit) is taken away. This means that all Spirit-filled believers (the Church) must be snatched away prior to the Tribulation, otherwise the Antichrist will not come to world prominence (2 Thess. 2:4-8).

Conclusion

There is a loss of imminency in the Mid-Tribulation rapture. With this mindset, the Church is not watching and waiting for the Lord, but for preparatory signs given to the nation of Israel announcing Jacob's time of trouble, Daniel's seventieth week. The emphasis of Bible prophecy for the midpoint of the Tribulation Period is the Abomination of Desolation (i.e., when the Antichrist breaks his covenant with Israel), not the rapture of the Church. The view is formed by the reference to the seventh trumpet judgment written of in Revelation and the last trump reference pertaining to the rapture in 1 Corinthians 15:51-52. However, the seventh trumpet is not the last trumpet blast to occur during the Tribulation Period, for the Jews will be summoned back to Israel at the conclusion of the Tribulation Period by the call of a trumpet.

Pre-Tribulation Rapture View

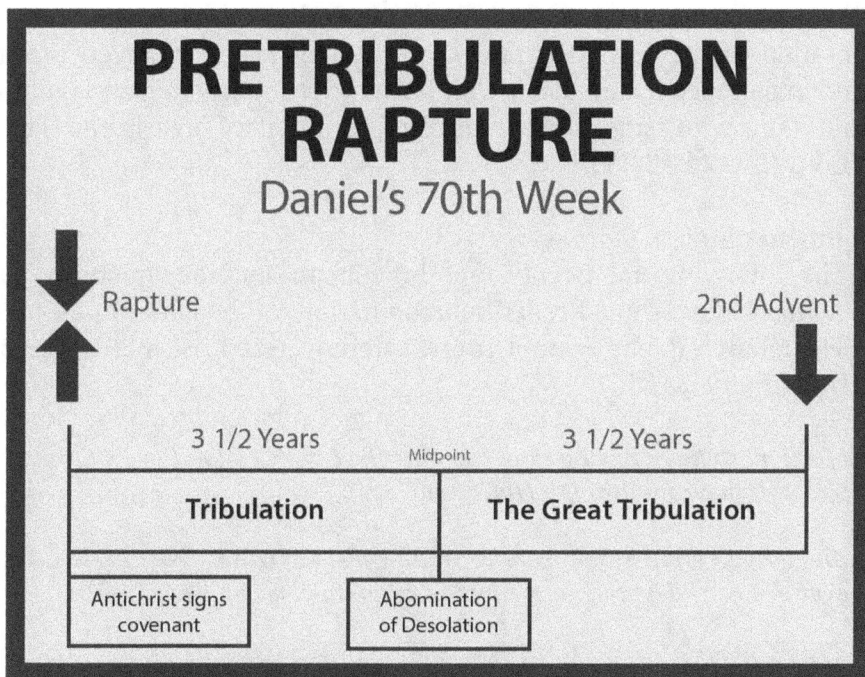

PRETRIBULATION RAPTURE
Daniel's 70th Week

Rapture

2nd Advent

3 1/2 Years Midpoint 3 1/2 Years

Tribulation	The Great Tribulation

Antichrist signs covenant	Abomination of Desolation

Christ will return from heaven to the air to remove His Church from the earth – this is the rapture. Seven years later, He will return to the earth with His saints to judge wickedness and establish His kingdom. Presently, Christ is seated on His Father's throne in heaven, but when He returns to the earth with His saints, He will establish His own throne and rule all the nations (Rev. 3:21).

It is the author's opinion that the Old Testament saints may be raised up with the Church prior to the Tribulation Period (Heb. 11:40). This position may be represented in Revelation 4 by the appearance of twenty-four crowned elders on twenty-four thrones situated around Christ in heaven. The number twenty-four is used in Scripture to symbolically speak of the priesthood (1 Chron. 24). Thus, it seems likely that the twenty-four elders, who are priests (Rev. 5:10) are associated with the twelve tribes of Israel and the twelve apostles of the Church, the gates and the foundations of the New Jerusalem, respectively (Rev. 21:12-14). Or, the Old Testament saints may be raised up with the tribulation saints at the end of the Tribulation Period, which aligns with the restoration of the Jewish nation. The prophet Isaiah believed that he would experience resurrection with His fellow countrymen and that this would align with Israel's spiritual restoration with Christ in the day of the Lord (Isa. 26:18-19).

Arguments For:

The following are twenty-four biblical reasons and pictures why this author believes in a Pre-Tribulation rapture of the Church:

1. The Church is not exempt from suffering for Christ, but is exempt from divine wrath:

   Much more then, having now been justified by His blood, we shall be saved from wrath through Him (Rom. 5:9).

   And to wait for His Son from heaven, whom He raised from the dead, even Jesus who delivers us from the wrath to come (1 Thess. 1:10).

   For God did not appoint us to wrath, but to obtain salvation through our Lord Jesus Christ (1 Thess. 5:9).

   God's wrath is against wickedness, not against His redeemed (Zech. 12:8-9). Therefore the Church must be taken to heaven before Christ opens the first seal on the scroll (Rev. 6:1) to initiate the Tribulation Period.

2. There is a time of great trouble coming called the Tribulation which will affect the entire world (Matt. 24:21). But as John acknowledges to the believers in the Church at Philadelphia, the Church will be brought home prior to its initiation: *"Because you have kept My command to persevere, I also will keep you from the hour of trial which shall come upon the whole world, to test those who dwell on the earth"* (Rev. 3:10). The Greek preposition *ek* is rightly translated "keep...from" in this verse; if the Lord were to preserve the Church *through* the Tribulation, the Greek preposition *dia* would be required. Although the Church will be taken to heaven before the

Tribulation Period, there is no promise of God to preserve Gentiles who turn to Christ after that event. In fact, many of those new believers will be slaughtered during the Tribulation Period (Rev. 7:9-14; 13:5).

3. The chronological order of events in Revelation uphold this view:
    *   Rev. 4:1-6:1: The Rapture, the Judgment seat of Christ
    *   Rev. 6-19: The Tribulation Period (as initiated by the Antichrist's political savvy in Rev. 6:1-2)
    *   Rev. 20: The Millennium
    *   Rev. 21-22: The Eternal State

4. The Church is seen coming back with the Lord to the earth at the end of the Tribulation Period (Rev. 19:14). The saints riding on horses have already received their crowns. Thus, the Lord must have previously come for the Church in order for the saints to be crowned in Revelation 4 (which occurs before the start of the Tribulation Period in Rev. 6:1). According to the Post-Tribulation rapture view, the Judgment Seat of Christ (where believers are rewarded) would have to occur at Christ's Second Advent to the earth, which means there would be no crowned saints in heaven before the Tribulation Period. The Tribulation Period does not start until Revelation 6, but the Church is already with Christ in heaven and wearing crowns in Revelation 4. Only a Pre-Tribulation Rapture view permits this timing to be realized.

5. Revelation 20:4 speaks of the resurrection of those killed during the Tribulation Period; these souls are seen in heaven (Rev. 6:9-11; 7:9-14). Their imprecatory prayers under God's altar in heaven demonstrate that they are not part of the Church, as the Holy Spirit within Christians prompts a passion for forgiveness, not vengeance (Rom. 12:17-20; Acts 7:60).

6. The attitude of the Apostles: they were looking for Christ not the Antichrist:

- John (AD 90): *"It is the last times"* (1 Jn. 2:18). *"He shall appear that we may have confidence and not be ashamed before Him at His coming"* (1 Jn. 2:28).
- Paul (AD 60): *"Then we who are alive and remain shall be caught up with Him"* (1 Thess. 4:17). *"We look for the Savior, the Lord Jesus, who shall change our lowly body, that it may be fashioned like His glorious body"* (Phil 3:20-21). *"We shall not all sleep, but we shall all be changed"* (1 Cor. 15:51).
- James (AD 45): *"The coming of the Lord draws near"* (Jas. 5:8).
- Peter (AD 66): *"That you be looking for the coming day of the Lord"* (2 Pet. 3:10-14). *"Christ's coming is at hand"* (2 Pet. 4:7).

7. The Jewish betrothal and marriage customs picture Christ coming for his Church prior to the Tribulation Period. In the historical Jewish betrothal custom, a man would approach a virgin's father to ask for her hand in marriage. If the father was agreeable to this, they would then negotiate the bride's price (i.e., the virgin's dowry). Once this had been finalized, the virgin's parents would have the prospective groom over for dinner. At this meal he would pour a glass of wine and offer it to the daughter, the prospective bride. If she accepted the glass from the suitor's hand, it meant that she accepted his proposal. If she did not accept the glass, his offer was rejected. If the marriage offer was accepted, the couple was then considered betrothed – they were bound by a marriage covenant. This began an interval called a "time of purity" in which the groom built a house near his father's house or added on a room to his father's house for him and his bride.

During this time of purity the bride was not idle either, for she was preparing her wedding gown and had to be ready to be called away by her husband when he came for her. Once the groom's father was satisfied that the new home was completely finished and furnished, he would instruct his son to go get his bride. When arriving at the bride's home, he would shout for her to come; she would quickly join him, and they would return together to the new home. After this, they enjoyed personal intimacy together, and then a marriage feast to celebrate their marriage and new home was held with their friends and relatives.

The parallels between Christ's relationship with the Church and that of the groom to the bride in the Jewish betrothal custom are impressive. When an individual accepts the gospel invitation, the dowry is applied (the blood Christ shed at Calvary). The night before He died, the Lord poured a glass of wine and gave it to His disciples to drink. He told them: *"This cup is the new testament in My blood, which is shed for you"* (Luke 22:20). They received it and drank it and a new covenant was acknowledged. Each time a believer drinks of the cup at the Lord's Supper, he is reaffirming "I do" to the Lord Jesus. The Lord promised His disciples later that evening that though He was leaving to prepare a place for them, He would return for them (John 14:2-3). When will the Lord come? While still on earth, the Lord admitted that only the Father knew (Matt. 24:36). So, the Son is busy preparing a home for His bride. When it is complete, the Father will tell His Son, "It is time to receive Your bride." The Church must always be ready for His sudden appearance to take her home, which means doing righteous works in the name of Christ, illustrated by the glorious gown of the bride (Rev. 3:18; 19:7-8).

8. Only 1 Corinthians 15:51-52 and 1 Thessalonians 4:13-18 reveal that there is a resurrection of the living and that this relates directly to the Church. Paul lived each day expecting this sudden transformation. At the rapture, our present sin-infested bodies will be renovated into sinless eternal bodies – bodies like Christ's glorified body (Phil. 3:20).
   - All other resurrections do not relate to the Church and occur after death. For example, Revelation 20:4 speaks of the resurrection of those killed during the Tribulation Period which occurs just prior to the Kingdom Age. The souls of these saints were in heaven during the Tribulation Period while they were waiting for bodily resurrection (Rev. 6:9-11; 7:9-14).

157

9. The One who hinders sin (i.e., Holy Spirit within believers) must be gone before Antichrist is revealed and begins his brief rule (2 Thess. 2:3-9). The Holy Spirit is the One who restrains the Antichrist, for *"greater is He that is in you, than he that is in the world"* (1 Jn. 4:4). When the Pre-Tribulation rapture of the Church occurs, every Spirit-indwelt believer will be removed from the earth. While the Holy Spirit will still be omnipresent and active, His special influence in the world through indwelt saints will be removed at the Rapture. While the Holy Spirit will continue to convict men of sin and their need for a Savior, the saints confronting evil with the message of the gospel and deeds of the gospel will no longer be present. One can only imagine how desperate the world scene will be after all those who have been born-again are snatched away (John 3:3).

10. Christ's Pre-Tribulation and Post-Tribulation appearances are described differently in Scripture:
    • Pre-Tribulation (1 Cor. 15:52): Christ meets the Church in the clouds and escorts her back to heaven, all of which happens in the twinkling of an eye. Christ does not come to the earth for this event and thus will be unseen by the masses.
    • Post-Tribulation (Matt. 24:27; Rev. 1:7): Everyone sees His coming to the earth.

11. The wholesale slaughter of believers during the Tribulation Period (Rev. 12:7, 15; 15:2; 20:4) shows that, at this point, God will have begun a new dispensation in human affairs (i.e., the Church Age will have concluded). Though the Church has been persecuted through the centuries, it has not been overcome because the Lord promised that it would not be (Matt. 16:18). On the other hand, there is no promise to protect anyone from the Antichrist's rage during the Tribulation Period, except for the 144,000 sealed Jewish representatives (Rev. 7:4-8) and a remnant of the Jewish nation (Rev. 12). Gentile believers during the Tribulation are slaughtered en masse (Rev. 6:9; 7:5, 14); these cannot be part of the Church, for Christ has promised to protect it.

12. Paul clearly taught that the Church would not go through the Day of the Lord, the Tribulation Period (1 Thess. 5:2-9). He spoke of non-believers as "they" and believers as "brethren," "you," "us," and "we." He then declared that the "brethren" would not be in the darkness of the Tribulation Period, but that non-believers would be.

13. The gospel message today is that Christ was crucified, buried, and resurrected so that we could be justified in Him and live in Him (1 Cor. 15:3-4). The gospel message preached to the Jews before Christ's death was the offering of a literal, earthly, political kingdom (Matt. 4:17). This offer was rejected, but will be made again during the Tribulation Period; this time, the Jewish nation will believe it (Matt. 24:1; Rev. 14:6, 9). The gospel message preached during different dispensations is always based in grace and must be trusted in by faith to make it effectual – though the exact message to be believed depends upon what stewardship God has placed on man at that time. During the Tribulation Period the inhabitants of the earth will be told not to worship the Antichrist, but rather fear and worship God, for judgment and Christ's kingdom is imminent.

14. The Kingdom Gospel is declared by angels (Luke 1:26-33; Rev. 14:6-10); however, during the Church Age only Christians have been entrusted to bear the gospel, not angels (Matt. 28:18-20; Acts 8:26). It is 144,000 Jews sealed during Tribulation that bear this message to *their brethren*, not Christians to the world (Rev. 7; Matt. 10:23).

15. The Church must be taken home for the Jews to be restored nationally unto God (Rom. 11:25; Ezek. 20:33-42; 39:25-29; Isa. 66); otherwise they would be added to the Church and Christ would have two physical temples on earth at the same time in Jerusalem and also in the non-glorified bodies of those composing the Church (Eph. 2:15-22). This creates confusion and there is no biblical example of God ever having two temples on earth at the same time.

16. Christ's exhortation to His disciples was to "watch" (Matt. 24:42) and "be ready" (Matt. 24:44). The Church was not to look for the

Antichrist or signs, but for Christ to come for them. Any Tribulation rapture view other than a Pre-Tribulation view has the Church watching and waiting for the Antichrist.

17. John did not know who the great multitude of believers were that had been brought into heaven from the Great Tribulation. John was told that these were those who had been martyred during the Great Tribulation for rejecting the Antichrist (Rev. 7:14). Obviously, these souls are not the raptured Church or John would have recognized some of his fellow believers. Since these souls are believers that were slaughtered during the Tribulation Period but had not experienced resurrection, and John did not know them, a previous resurrection of the Church before the Tribulation Period must have occurred. The Tribulation saints of Revelation 7 do not experience resurrection until after Satan is bound in a bottomless pit and Christ is ruling on earth (Rev. 19:20-20:4).

18. The Church is mentioned specifically over one hundred times in the New Testament and referred to many more times indirectly. It is noted that the Church is not specifically mentioned from Revelation 3:22 until Revelation 22:16 and that the Tribulation Period is addressed from Revelation 6:1-19:21. Given how important the Church is, it's inconceivable that it would be on earth for the Tribulation and yet not even be mentioned in all the chapters describing the Tribulation.

19. As before mentioned, the Lord ascended into heaven as the King of Glory after His resurrection. The Lord responds to the heavenly sentinel's question, *"Who is the King of Glory?"* with this statement: *"The Lord strong and mighty, the Lord mighty in battle"* (Ps. 24:8). At Calvary, the Lord defeated the prince of the world (John 12:31) and death itself (Rev. 1:18; John 10:17-18). His Father welcomed Him into heaven, highly exalted Him, and set Him at His right hand (Heb. 1:3; Rev. 3:21). Later, Christ will leave this privileged position briefly to return to the earth's atmosphere to gather up His Church (Ps. 24:9). Thus, at His second entrance to heaven He will not be alone; He informs the sentinel that He is *"the*

King of Glory – the Lord of hosts" (Ps. 24:10). The fact that the Lord returns to heaven with His beloved bride ensures that a Post-Tribulation rapture of the Church at Christ's Second Advent to the earth could not occur.

20. Because of persecution, Paul was forced to depart Thessalonica shortly after preaching the gospel and establishing a local church there. Paul wrote his first epistle to these new believers after arriving in Corinth. He taught them about the Day of Christ (i.e., the rapture of the Church and the Judgment Seat of Christ). This event would result in the resurrection of dead believers and the transformation of living believers into glorified bodies in order to be with Christ in heaven (John 14:1-4; 1 Cor. 15:51-52; Phil. 3:20-21). An individual's soul is saved when he or she trusts in Christ alone for salvation, but at the rapture, the believer's body will be saved from the presence of sin. This is an event which believers are to exceedingly yearn for and thus it is always presented in a positive way in Scripture (1 Cor. 1:8; 3:13; 5:5; Phil. 1:6, 10). Directly after teaching them about the rapture of the Church, which they were to expect (1 Thess. 4:13-18), Paul informed them of the next event, "the Day of the Lord," which he equated to the Tribulation Period (1 Thess. 5:1-5). Paul told the believers that they would not participate in this day (1 Thess. 5:4). This order of revelation again confirms a Pre-Tribulation rapture of the Church – the Day of the Lord must follow the Day of Christ!

Old Testament Pictures of the Pre-Tribulation Rapture

1. **The life of Enoch.** Apparently, Enoch's conversion was about the time of his son Methuselah's birth. Enoch was 65 years old when Methuselah was born. In a mysterious way, the birth of his son was a prophecy in itself – Methuselah's name means "when it comes." God was telling Enoch that as long as his son lived, the world would live, but when his son died, the world would die. How do you think this knowledge affected Enoch's life? He did not know when his son would die, so he had to live in constant anticipation of suddenly being ushered into the presence of God.

161

When did Methuselah die? Methuselah was 187 years old when his son Lamech was born, and Lamech was 182 years old when Noah was born. Noah was 600 years old when the flood came (Gen. 7:6). Consequently, Methuselah was 969 years old when the flood came and Scripture records that he lived 969 years. He died the year the flood occurred. Enoch pictures the Church living by faith, walking with God, and then being translated before the wrath of God on the wicked. We read in Hebrews 11:5 that Enoch was translated without seeing death. What a beautiful picture of the rapture of the Church as described by Paul (1 Thess. 4:13-18; 1 Cor. 15:51-52). Likewise, the Church is to operate today with the anticipation of suddenly being ushered into the presence of God. This is the hope of the Church: *"Looking for that blessed hope, and the glorious appearing of the great God and our Savior, Jesus Christ"* (Titus 2:13). The Lord's return may not be immediate, but it is imminent!

2. **The life of Noah.** Noah and his family entered into the ark, a type of Christ, and escaped the wrath of God upon all the wicked of the earth (Gen. 6-9). The fact that Methuselah lived longer than any other man in the Bible illustrates God's longsuffering nature. Second Peter 3:9 reads, *"The Lord is not slack concerning His promise, as some men count slackness, but is longsuffering toward us, not willing that any should perish, but that all should come to repentance."* The Lord was longsuffering because a righteous man was preaching repentance to the people. Who was this righteous preacher? Noah. We learn from 1 Peter 3:18-20 and 2 Peter 2:5 that Christ was preaching through Noah to the wicked men of earth. This preaching lasted until the ark was completed. Every gopher tree felled, every sound of wood being gnawed by a saw or chopped by ax, and every pound of the hammer was a call to repentance and gave testimony that judgment was coming. In the end, only eight souls were saved from God's wrath because they entered the ark that they had built by faith. Their faith was based solely on the Word of God – no signs were given to Noah to believe. This is noteworthy since Israel has been given many prophetic signs, but the Church has not been.

The ark itself is a type of Christ. In the broad sense, the ark pictures the safety that Christ offers all who will "enter in" the Church by faith. Before the ark could be constructed, building materials were needed – gopher trees had to be cut down. The death of these trees pictured the humanity of Christ in that only through His sacrifice could spiritual life for man be secured. But since trees don't have blood, God is careful to apply some to the ark that we not miss the type. The word "pitch" in Genesis 6:14 is most often translated "atonement" (nearly 75 times in the Old Testament). Prior to Calvary, man's sin could only be atoned for (covered) by the blood of animals through sacrifices. The fact that the ark was pitched from within and without further foreshadows the future suffering and sacrifice of Christ. From His wounds, redemptive blood would rudely and profusely coat his outer skin and then drip and splatter upon the ground. The word usage and the typology of Genesis 6 both convey the visage of a bleeding ark, thus picturing the suffering Savior at Calvary.

There was only one door into the ark (Gen. 6:16), and only God could shut it (Gen. 7:16) once all those who entered by faith were within. It would be God who judged the earth for man's wickedness (Gen. 6:7); thus, the very ark that Noah had built would know God's wrath. However, while the ark bore the judgment of almighty God, all the souls that were in the ark were kept safe from judgment. The Lord Jesus said He was the only door (John 10:1) and the only way (John 14:6), and He bore the judgment of God for man's sin once and for all (Heb. 9:26-28; 10:9-18). The Lord said, *"whosoever lives and believes in Me shall never die"* (John 11:26). Our souls' security rests in the hand (John 10:28-29) and the sealing power of God (Eph. 1:13). We never read of water pouring through the door to despair Noah's family or that any family member was lost at sea. When God sealed the door shut, it was securely closed, and when God seals the believer in Christ, he or she is maintained securely within and is saved from God's wrath to come.

3. **The life of Isaac** (Gen. 21-25). The miracle birth of Isaac in Genesis 21, the promised son to elderly Abraham and Sarah,

pictures the incarnation of the only begotten Son of God (Heb. 11:6, 17). Later, Genesis 22 records the journey of Abraham to a mount in Moriah to sacrifice Isaac, as God requested. This pictures the then future act of God the Father judging His innocent Son at this location some two thousand years later. After Abraham's love for the Lord was proven, a ram was substituted for Isaac. Sarah dies in Genesis 23. As previously mentioned, she is the only woman in the Bible to have her age recorded at death and there is a reason – to show how long Isaac mourned his mother's death. He married Rebekah at the age of forty and was comforted (Gen. 24:67; 25:20). This means he grieved for three years, which is also the timeframe that the Lord Jesus preached to the nation of Israel and grieved over their spiritual deadness (Luke 13:7).

Sarah, who pictures Israel (e.g. Israel is the woman who bore the only begotten son in Rev. 12:1-2), was buried in the cave of Machpelah near Hebron. The Hebrew root word for "Hebron" comes from *cheber*, which means "a society or a fellowship." The Hebrew root word for "Machpelah" is derived from *kaphal*, which means "to fold together," or by implication, "to repeat" or "to double." Exodus 19:5 and Psalm 135:4 inform us that God considers Israel a treasure for Himself. It seems, then, that what is pictured here in Sarah's death is the spiritual death of the nation of Israel (they were cut off from God), which occurred after the offering of the Son (Gen. 22), but before the wooing of a Gentile bride for the Son (Gen. 24). A "society" and a "treasure" were, thus, hidden again in the world, a second time or a "double" time (see Matt. 13:44). However, at the Lord's Second Coming, He will be accepted by the Jewish nation (Zech. 12:10), and they will then receive the Holy Spirit and be restored unto God as His people. The events surrounding Sarah's death, the fact that she was buried in a cave, that the cave was called Machpelah and was near Hebron convey a prophetic portrait of God's future dealing with the nation of Israel.

When Sarah died, the marriage covenant with Abraham was severed (Rom. 7:1-6); this event was followed by a marriage covenant instituted in Genesis 24 between Isaac and Rebekah, thus portraying the New Covenant in Christ's blood, which put away the Old Covenant. The unnamed servant in Genesis 24 pictures the Holy Spirit who at this moment is wooing a Gentile bride for Christ. The death of Sarah allows Abraham to receive a new wife in Genesis 25 (Keturah) after Isaac is joined to Rebekah. As Sarah's resurrection was not a possibility, Abraham's subsequent marriage with Keturah, who bore him six sons, is used to depict the future restoration of a refined and fruitful Jewish nation with Jehovah. This event occurs after the church is in heaven with Christ (Isaac and Rebekah were joined together in Genesis 24). The Old Covenant had its strength in the law, which could not be kept and, thus, brought death, but the New Covenant is empowered by God's grace through Christ's blood. As a result, the New Covenant brought salvation to both Jew and Gentile (Luke 22:20; Eph. 3:6-7). The typological focus of Isaac representing Christ concludes in Genesis 25:5 when Abraham dies and Isaac inherits all that his father had – this speaks of the Kingdom Age.

4. **The Feasts of Jehovah** (Lev. 23). To prevent the Israelite's love for Him from growing cold, Jehovah instituted several reminders for them to observe: annual feasts (Ex. 34:18, 22-23), the redemption of the firstborn (of man and beast; Ex. 34:19-20), and the Sabbath Day (Ex. 34:21; 35:1-3). In Exodus 34, more details are provided to Moses concerning the Feasts of Jehovah. Three seasons of festivals, including a total of seven feasts, were to be observed by the Israelites. Every Jewish male was required to present himself before Jehovah three times a year at the Feast of Unleavened Bread, the Feast of Weeks, and the Feast of Ingathering.

Leviticus 23 identifies all seven of the Feasts of Jehovah. These feasts provide an exceptional prophetic blueprint of God's means of reconciling the nation of Israel to Himself forever. Every aspect of this blueprint centers in the work of Christ:

Passover (14th day of 1st month) pictures Christ on the cross on Friday; this was the day the Passover lambs were slain and was also the day when the Lamb of God was slain for the sins of the world (1 Cor. 5:7).

Unleavened Bread (15th day of 1st month) speaks of Christ in the grave on Saturday; like the bread, Christ's body had neither life while in the grave nor had it been previously influenced by sin (i.e., Christ lived an unleavened life).

First Fruits (16th day of the 1st month) typifies Christ's resurrection on Sunday; He was the first fruits from the dead (1 Cor. 15:20).

Pentecost (fifty days after First Fruits) pictures the formation of the Church (Christ's body of believers) fifty days after Christ's resurrection. The events at Pentecost conveyed a final ultimatum to Israel (Acts 2).

Note: The Church Age is represented by the gap between the Spring and Autumn feasts (this also relates to the interval between Daniel's 69th and 70th weeks; Dan. 9:24-27). The Autumn feasts speak of Israel's future acknowledgement of Christ as Messiah, their restoration to Him, and the blessings of His Millennial Kingdom.

Trumpets (1st day of the 7th month) refers to the time when Christ will gather all the Jews back to Israel and under His rule (Matt. 24:29-31; Ezek. 39:28-29).

The Day of Atonement (10th day of the 7th month) pictures the future event when the Jews will repent and receive Jesus Christ as their Messiah (Heb. 9:28; Zech. 12:10).

Tabernacles (15th day of the 7th month) announces the future release of the Jews from the Antichrist's rule during the Tribulation Period, and the blessings of Christ's rule during His Millennial Kingdom.

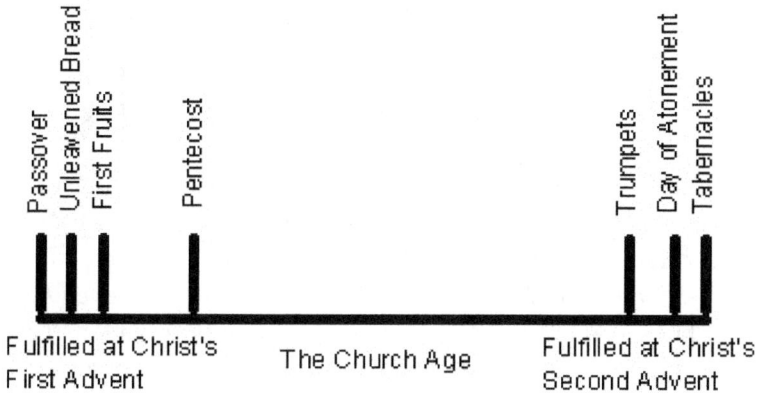

God indeed has a wonderful plan for the nation of Israel. Prophetically speaking, the spring feasts are completed, while the fall feasts are yet to be fulfilled. When the last trumpet of the Tribulation Period is heard, every Jew will be gathered out of the nations back to the land of Israel; this refined remnant will then receive the Holy Spirit (Ezek. 39:28-29).

Conclusion

It is this author's conviction that only a Pre-Tribulation Rapture of the Church fully satisfies the revelation of all Scripture. The Lord Jesus does not want His Church to be looking for signs of His coming (those are for Israel) or for the appearance of the Antichrist, but rather to be watching and waiting for Him in a personal sense. All those who live with the hope of His imminent return will receive a reward at His coming (2 Tim. 4:8). Practically speaking, believers who truly long for the Lord's coming will flee sin and loath worldliness since they do not want to be caught with their hand in the cookie jar, so to speak, if He were to suddenly appear (1 Jn. 3:3).

Does the Church have the "hope of glory"? Yes, we agree with Paul and Peter's assessment:

To them God willed to make known what are the riches of the glory of this mystery among the Gentiles: which is Christ in you, the hope of glory (Col. 1:27).

Blessed be the God and Father of our Lord Jesus Christ, who according to His abundant mercy has begotten us again to a living hope through the resurrection of Jesus Christ from the dead, to an inheritance incorruptible and undefiled and that does not fade away, reserved in heaven for you, who are kept by the power of God through faith for salvation ready to be revealed in the last time (1 Pet. 1:3-5).

The Church has a living hope, the rapture, the coming of the Lord Jesus Christ to the air to snatch the Church from the earth: *"Then we which are alive and remain shall be caught up together with them in the clouds, to meet the Lord in the air: and so shall we ever be with the Lord"* (1 Thess. 4:17). Dead believers will undergo resurrection. All believers, living and dead, will at that moment experience glorification. This is the culmination of our salvation and permits us to be in the presence of the Lord Jesus Christ forever!

> In hope we lift our wishful, longing eyes,
> Waiting to see the Morning Star arise;
> How bright, how gladsome will His advent be,
> Before the Sun shines forth in majesty!
>
> How will our eyes to see His face delight,
> Whose love has cheered us through the darksome night!
> How will our ears drink in His well-known voice,
> Whose faintest whispers make our soul rejoice!
>
> — James G. Deck

The Believer's Hope –
To Be With Christ

A Body Fit for Heaven

C. H. Spurgeon, the prince of preachers, once received a copy of Andrew Bonar's *Commentary on Leviticus*. It so blessed him that he returned the book to the author and requested the following favor: "Dr. Bonar, please place herein your autograph and your photograph." The book was returned to him with the following note from Dr. Bonar: "Dear Spurgeon, here is the book with my autograph and with my photograph. If you had been willing to wait a short season, you could have had a better likeness, for I shall be like Him; I shall see Him as He is (1 Jn. 3:2)."[1] Dr. Bonar understood that there was a time coming when his appearance would be much more pleasant to the beholder. Why? Because after experiencing resurrection, believers will perfectly reflect the glory of Christ to all who behold them. Although still appearing different from each other, the outshining of God's glory will characterize all those in heaven.

The Lord's Body

Some of what we learn about glorified bodies is presented to us in the testimonies of those who saw the Lord after His resurrection. The Lord Jesus remained on earth to encourage and instruct His disciples for forty days after His resurrection. His first appearance to them was quite a shocker. The disciples, for fear of the Jews, had gathered together in secret behind locked doors when, suddenly, the Lord stood in their midst (John 20:19). Not only could He pass through solid objects, but He also knew right where the disciples were. After examining the Lord's hands and His side, the disciples were completely convinced that the One before them was He that had been crucified three days earlier. This was one of five separate eye-witness accounts of the Lord on the very day He was raised from the dead. Scripture contains five more personal testimonies of the Lord's physical presence before His ascension into heaven. Paul states that on one such occasion, more than 500 believers saw Him (1 Cor. 15:6).

The Lord Jesus prophesied His own resurrection (John 2:19-21; Acts 2:26-27) and showed His disciples His resurrected body (Luke 24:40; John 20:27). When He first met with the disciples after His resurrection, the Lord told them He was not a spirit, but flesh and bone (Luke 24:39). He then ate some fish and honeycomb in their presence (Luke 24:42). By showing the nail prints in His body to the disciples, the Lord Jesus demonstrated that the body He now had was the same body that had been nailed to the cross.

While it is true that the Lord kept some of His disciples from immediately recognizing Him after His resurrection (this was for teaching purposes), most of them clearly recognized the Lord when He appeared before them. We can therefore conclude that the Lord's glorified body was much like His pre-resurrection body in appearance. His resurrected body could taste food, could be touched, and could be seen and heard; it also could instantly vanish and reappear elsewhere (Luke 24:37-39). So while His body exhibited some properties of natural law, it also possessed supernatural qualities. Same body, but different. To illustrate this idea, I might show an old friend a picture of my son at a young age and another picture of him ten years later to highlight his growth during that time. Although it is a picture of the same person and of the same body, many features of that body had changed while other features were similar. The Lord's resurrected body was the same one He had had previously, but it was vastly different.

When the Lord experienced resurrection, His body was changed. He still could be recognized by others, but His body was quite different than the one He possessed before. We need blood pumping throughout our bodies to stay alive, but the Lord had no blood in His body – that was shed at Calvary for you and me. The Lord's body was flesh and bone. His glorified body did not require natural metabolic operations to sustain it as our bodies do. In fact, Paul says, *"That flesh and blood cannot inherit the kingdom of God"* (1 Cor. 15:50). Obviously, the laws of existence in heaven are quite different from those our bodies on earth operate within; thus, our present bodies are not fit for heaven.

The Glorified Body

Have you ever wondered what kind of body believers will have in heaven? There were some in Paul's day who pondered this same question. Unfortunately, some of these individuals began to question the teaching of resurrection because they could not understand how a physical body could exist in heaven. Paul uses a horticultural example to explain this difficulty.

Just as a seed must fall into the ground and die in order to bring forth life, we must die to experience resurrection (i.e., when a seed is sown, there is an expectation of something rising from that location later). Our future resurrected bodies will draw characteristics from our earthly bodies in the same way a corn plant acquires its characteristics from the kernel of corn that was sown (1 Cor. 15:36-38). The plant is not the seed per se, but what it is was drawn from the seed. This seems to indicate that the individuality of our human soul will be maintained in heaven, though our visible form will be quite different.

Paul says that our present bodies are perishable, weak, and natural; however, our glorified bodies will be imperishable, powerful, and spiritual (1 Cor. 15:51-53). The former often dishonors the Lord, but that would be impossible with the latter body – there is no flesh nature within it to cause the glorified body to rebel against the Lord. John states that believers will have a body like the Lord Jesus' body, which obviously cannot commit sin: *"Beloved, now we are children of God; and it has not yet been revealed what we shall be, but we know that when He is revealed, we shall be like Him, for we shall see Him as He is"* (1 Jn. 3:2). Paul describes the same truth: *"For our citizenship is in heaven, from which we also eagerly wait for the Savior, the Lord Jesus Christ, who will transform our lowly body that it may be conformed to His glorious body, according to the working by which He is able even to subdue all things to Himself"* (Phil. 3:20-21). Having a Christ-like body in heaven means that everyone will morally act like God forever. There will be no ill thoughts about other people, no crippling bents, no temptations, nor will there be any addictions with which to grapple. God is a holy God and to dwell in His presence we will have to be holy too.

Paul states that the appearing of the Lord Jesus is the blessed hope of the Church (Titus 2:11) and that those who love the Lord's appearing (i.e., live as if the Lord could come back at any moment) will be rewarded for doing so (2 Tim. 4:8). John says that those who live expectantly for Christ's return will live purely, because the Lord is pure and because a believer would not want to be ashamed when He does suddenly come for His people (1 Jn. 2:28; 3:3). So although believers have not received their resurrection bodies yet, we are to live as though we have!

As the believer's flesh nature will be eradicated, the present needs and desires of our bodies will cease to exist. There will be no need for air, water, food, rest, sleep, or reproduction. The upshot is that perfect bodies will not need eyeglasses, wheelchairs, hearing aids, pacemakers, dentures, hormone therapies, pain medications, sleep aids, etc. Doesn't heaven sound great?

Clothing for Heaven

Have you ever wondered how people will be attired in heaven? What will those born again in Christ be wearing? The Lord Jesus rebuked the Church at Laodicea with these words: *"You are wretched, miserable, poor, blind, and naked – I counsel you to buy from Me gold refined in the fire, that you may be rich; and white garments, that you may be clothed, that the shame of your nakedness may not be revealed; and anoint your eyes with eye salve, that you may see"* (Rev. 3:17-18). Those in the Church at Laodicea were not living for Christ; consequently, God's righteousness was not displayed in their lives. While all believers in the Church have been positionally declared righteous in Christ, each believer has the opportunity to labor in righteousness for Christ. Those things which are done in accordance with revealed truth and in the power of the Holy Spirit have eternal value; these righteous acts are what the believer is adorned with throughout eternity. In heaven, the bride of Christ must have righteous attire; she is *"arrayed in fine linen, clean and bright, for the fine linen is the righteous acts of the saints"* (Rev. 19:8).

Paul explains in 1 Corinthians 15:40-42 that after the resurrection, some saints will shine forth the glory of God more brightly than others, just as some stars in the nighttime sky are brighter than other stars. This acquired glory directly reflects the righteous acts (good works) that are done for Christ by His strength in this present life. Eternal glory, evidently, has a weight to it; in other words, its quality is measurable (2 Cor. 4:17) and can be earned by believers through selfless service for Christ now. Thus, to be appropriately dressed for eternity, believers should secure for themselves a covering of eternal glory, which consists of righteous acts. Though saved, a believer may still appear to be spiritually naked in heaven (i.e., personal acts of righteousness on earth provide believers with varying reflections of God's glory in heaven: Rev. 3:18; 1 Cor. 15:41-42; 2 Cor. 4:17). Without being justified in Christ, no one can enter into heaven. Similarly, only by doing righteous acts for Him and by His power do believers contribute to their eternal attire of glory.

Though believers in heaven will reflect the glory of God in varying degrees, all the redeemed will be wearing white robes and have human form (Rev. 4:4; 19:14). Even before the martyred Tribulation saints experience glorification after the Tribulation Period (Rev. 20:4), they are described as wearing white robes in heaven (Rev. 6:11; 7:9, 13). The white robes represent divine purity and each believer's righteous position in Christ.

All will be wearing the same thing, there will be no unusual outward qualities to attract the attention of someone else, nor will we have the desire to respond to such things anyway. In the book of Revelation, except for two occasions when one of the twenty-four elders speaks to John, whenever those in heaven do speak, it is in unison and to praise and worship God. One of the great blessings of heaven will be this ability to honor God corporately with one voice, which again alleviates the possibility of any believer calling attention to himself or herself.

What is delightful and precious about everyone in heaven is that they will shine forth the glory of God and desire to worship and to honor Him in everything they do. What makes heaven heaven is that the One who suffered and died for me will be there – anything that draws attention away from Him would be an intolerable distraction: *My Beloved is mine, and I am His*" (SOS 2:16).

175

What Will Heaven Be Like?

A young city girl was in the country for the first time and, looking up into the night sky, commented, "Oh, mother, if heaven is so beautiful on the wrong side, what must it be like on the right side!"[1] Indeed, how can we possibly know what God's dwelling place is like unless He tells us about it or provides us some glimpse of it? In fact, God has been providing mankind with links between heaven and earth for millennia in order to assist our understanding of His abode.

God used prophetic visions and dreams, angelic visits, and preincarnate appearances of the Son of God to open our understanding of heavenly things. Most of these are recorded in the Old Testament. For example, Isaiah saw a vision of God and His heavenly throne room (Isa. 6:1-8); also in a vision, Ezekiel saw the Lord, His throne, and heavenly creatures about it (Ezek. 1). Then, there are the personal testimonies of people such as Elisha, who watched his mentor, Elijah, ascend into heaven in a fiery chariot (2 Kgs. 2:1-11), and Moses, who, on the mount, witnessed incredible sights beyond this world.

In the New Testament, Paul was caught up into the third heaven (God's spiritual domain) and saw things that he could not speak of (2 Cor. 12:2-4). John was also taken up into heaven and told to write down what he saw (Rev. 4:1-2) even though there were a few things that he was instructed not to record (Rev. 10:4). All this is to say that there is a good deal of biblical information which allows us to understand what God wants us to comprehend about heaven. What He has not revealed to us, we are not responsible to understand, nor is it likely that we could anyway (Deut. 29:29; Amos 4:13).

When John wrote the book of Revelation, he was an old man who had been banished to the Isle of Patmos by the Roman government. He was spiritually caught up into heaven to preview the prophetic messages that he was to write down (Rev. 1:1, 10; 4:1-2). Paul, on the other hand, when transported into God's presence, did not know whether he was in or out of his body. Yet he was fully conscious of the Lord's presence, and allowed to see and hear sacred things, though he was not permitted to speak of them to others. What is clear from Paul's experience and should be an encouragement to all believers is that though he did not know what form he was in while in heaven, he was fully aware of the Lord's presence there. This tells us that whether the believer's soul is in heaven before or after his or her resurrection occurs, the Lord's presence will be enjoyed in either case (2 Cor. 5:8; Phil. 1:23). Being with the Lord is the thrill of heaven and what all true believers long for.

What, then, does heaven look like? Much of what the Bible tells us of heaven is in metaphors. We need to be careful how we interpret the meanings of biblical symbols. Thankfully, the Bible, which was written over a 1,600-year period by about forty different writers, employs a consistent use of symbols throughout its framework. By applying the observed meanings of symbols used throughout Scripture, we can understand what God wants us to know about heaven.

Moses was to construct the tabernacle and its furnishings according to the pattern that God showed him, which was a mere shadow (an abstract copy, if you will) of the heavenly things which already existed (Heb. 8:5). John was also shown heavenly things through the use of symbolic depiction (Rev. 1:1). Besides the divine message contained in the Bible's narrative, God also uses numbers, symbols, metals, colors, names, etc. to convey information. These more abstract forms of revelation do not alter the clear teaching of Scripture, but rather reiterate the message through metaphor. When God initially introduces an object, a number, a color, etc. in a metaphoric presentation, that symbolic meaning is held consistently throughout all sixty-six books of the Bible.

For example, let us briefly consider the subject of numerology. In Scripture, the numbers one through forty are used in a consistent way when a metaphoric meaning is intended. Though most numbers in Scripture have a literal meaning, some numbers also serve a figurative purpose. The Lord Jesus, the Lamb, is described as having seven horns before the throne of God in Revelation 5:6. I don't believe that the Lord Jesus Christ will physically look like this in heaven. Rather, the seven horns symbolically represent His omnipotence, as seven is used throughout Scripture as the number of perfection, while a horn represents power. He is also described in the same verse as having seven eyes. Since eyes are for seeing, we understand this description to speak of the Lord's divine omniscience – He knows and sees all things.

The consistent use of symbols, numbers, analogies, names, first-mention occurrences, fulfilled prophetic types and shadows, plus the plain and consistent teachings of the Bible prove it to be the orchestrated genius of one great Mind. It stands to reason, then, that we must learn the meanings of several biblical symbols to better understand heaven as shown to us in the book of Revelation. I will highlight some of these as we think together about heaven.

God's Throne

John was permitted to see God's throne in heaven and records what he saw in Revelation 4. In that chapter, John mentions the throne of God twelve times and is careful not to describe anything else he saw except in its relationship to the throne. To emphasize this connection, Jim Flanigan observes John's use of five prepositional clauses:

- *Upon the Throne* – Deity sitting in inscrutable splendor.
- *Round about the Throne* – a rainbow, twenty-four crowned elders, and four strange living creatures.
- *Out of the Throne* – lightning, thundering, and voices.
- *Before the Throne* – seven lamps of fire, a sea of glass, and the proffered crowns of the elders.
- *In the midst of the Throne* – the four living ones, who also surround the Throne; and ... the Lamb (Rev. 5).[2]

In summary, nothing is described in this heavenly scene apart from its connection with God's throne. Why? Because God is sovereign over all things and is accountable to nobody. Everything that exists is dependent upon Him. Without God upon His throne, nothing else would matter. This is why the first sight that John describes after being caught up into heaven by the Holy Spirit was God upon His throne:

And He who sat there was like a jasper and a sardius stone in appearance; and there was a rainbow around the throne, in appearance like an emerald. Around the throne were twenty-four thrones, and on the thrones I saw twenty-four elders sitting, clothed in white robes; and they had crowns of gold on their heads. And from the throne proceeded lightnings, thunderings, and voices, seven lamps of fire were burning before the throne, which are the seven Spirits of God (Rev. 4:3-5).

The priority of what John describes is important. Some think that it will be streets of gold, foundations of precious stones, and pearly gates that will make heaven special; however, heaven would not be a spectacular domain at all if God were not there. John, thus, begins his revelation with the most spectacular sight in heaven – God Himself upon His throne.

John describes the outshining of God's holy essence – His spectacular glory. The prophet relates this visible manifestation of God's essence to the colors reflected from a jasper and a sardius stone. Jasper is used twice in Revelation 21 as a symbol of God's glory in connection with the New Jerusalem, God's eternal heavenly city (Rev. 21:10-11). In fact, the walls of this city are made entirely of jasper (Rev. 21:18). Jasper is a crystalline form of silica containing fine minerals of quartz and moganite. It is neither transparent nor translucent, meaning that all visible light reaching its surface is either absorbed or reflected back to us in the colors red, yellow, brown, green, and sometimes blue. Sardius is a red stone. There is no form upon the throne to describe, only a dazzling spectacle of various hues of light emanating from it. It is noted that sardius and jasper were the first and the last precious stones, respectively, in the High Priest's breastplate (Ex. 28:17-20). These two stones mentioned in tandem, then, may be a picture of God's immutable and eternal glory.

John also saw a rainbow encircling the throne. God promised Noah that He would never destroy the earth again by water; the rainbow was given to mankind as a symbol of that covenant. The circle never stops and thus represents eternity. The compound symbol indicates that God's promises are eternal – He is a covenant-keeping God.

Around God's throne were twenty-four other thrones upon which twenty-four elders were seated. The elders represent the redeemed just resurrected from the earth, which certainly would include, but may not be limited to, the Church (Rev. 5:9). These were clothed in white raiment and were wearing gold crowns upon their heads (Rev. 4:4). These crowns, or rewards, are given by the Lord Jesus Christ to His saints for their honorable service to Him. Though there are likely many other types of crowns given to reward faithfulness, five are mentioned in Scripture:

The Crown of Glory will be given to church elders who shepherd well (1 Pet. 5:4).
The Crown of Life will be given to those who endure trials because they love the Lord (Jas. 1:12).
The Crown of Rejoicing will be given to those who are soul-winners for Christ (1 Thess. 2:19; Phil 4:1); this crown may be more encompassing, such as a reward for contributing to spiritual growth in general.
The Crown of Righteousness will be given to those who long for His appearing (2 Tim. 4:8).
The Incorruptible Crown will be given to those who control fleshly desires through the Holy Spirit (1 Cor. 9:25).

The rewards that are earned during this lifetime provide the believer with a greater appreciation for the Lord, a greater capacity to worship Him throughout eternity, and, indeed, a greater capability to enjoy heaven (Rev. 4:11).

As both the twelve apostles and the twelve tribes of Israel are clearly tied to the New Jerusalem in Revelation 21, it is my opinion that the same numerical representation of twenty-four is used here to express that all those who have been redeemed up until this point in time have experienced glorification (Rev. 5:8-10). This would include the Old Testament saints, who were mainly connected with the nation of Israel, and the Church in the New Testament (Heb. 11:40). The Lord Jesus told His disciples that they would be seated about Him on twelve thrones in a future day. *"Assuredly I say to you, that in the regeneration, when the Son of Man sits on the throne of His glory, you who have followed Me will also sit on twelve thrones, judging the twelve tribes of Israel"* (Matt. 19:28). The scene of Revelation 4 and 5 shows that the Lord Jesus is on His Father's throne (Rev. 3:21); that is, He is still waiting to establish His kingdom on earth. At that time, He will sit on His own throne in Jerusalem. The twenty-four elders on their thrones in heaven are also anticipating their opportunity to rule and reign with Christ in His kingdom.

The elders in this scene have already been rewarded for faithful service and seated in a place of honor about the throne of God and the Lamb. This refers to the Judgment Seat of Christ, which occurs immediately after the Rapture of the Church from the earth (1 Cor. 3:11-15; 2 Cor. 5:10; Rom. 14:12-14). This is a remarkable scene as humans were created to govern the world, not heaven, and humans have a lower position in creation than the angels (Gen. 1:26; Heb. 2:6-8). Yet we never read of angels seated on thrones in Scripture, nor do they rule and reign with Christ as redeemed humanity will; they were created as eternal beings to serve God and will remain unchanged forever.

John observed that there was continual lightning, thunder, and voices proceeding out from God's throne. This description creates an unsettling disposition about the scene. We are left wondering if this ominous panorama depicts God's throne presently or relates to the future period which John was observing. William Kelly answers this quandary:

> Do thunderings and lightnings and voices proceed from the throne of God at this present time? …Certainly not. The throne of God now is a throne of grace, to which we come boldly (Heb. 4:14-16). …Clearly the thunderings and lightnings and voices are the expression of God's displeasure and judicial feeling, so to speak, towards things and people upon the earth.[3]

That this scene represents the future reality of looming worldwide judgment seems to be a logical conclusion given the testimony of Scripture as a whole. Once in fellowship with God, Moses and the elders of Israel ate a meal before the Lord's throne on Mt. Sinai and all was quiet (Ex. 24:9-12). Neither Stephen nor Paul mentioned anything about thunder, lightning, and voices during their glimpses of God's throne during the Church Age. But on the eve of pouring out judgment on the wicked, His throne rumbles.

Before the throne are seven torches which are identified with the Spirit of God. The number seven, as earlier mentioned, is God's number and represents perfection, completeness, and holiness. The lampstand in the tabernacle and the temple was patterned after this very scene. Through the number seven, the light of the lampstand (representing Christ's testimony of truth) is shown to be divine in origin. Similarly, the resource enabling the seven flames to illuminate the tabernacle (the oil) is also shown to be divine in nature. As in Zechariah's vision of the two olive trees that supplied oil to a lampstand, the Holy Spirit is depicted in the pure oil. Speaking of the oil, the Lord told Zechariah: *"Not by might nor by power, but by My Spirit"* (Zech. 4:6). The lampstand in the tabernacle, then, speaks of God's perfect revelation of truth in Christ through the power of the Holy Spirit.

Returning to Revelation 6, the next detail John describes in relationship to God's throne is the sea of glass before it. The laver in the tabernacle and the temple was patterned after this crystal sea, yet these earthly lavers held water, not glass, so a clear distinction is being made between the type and the antitype, as seen by John. Why the difference? As long as there was a Christian on earth, the practical aspects of cleaning defilement from the believer's life would be a necessary ministry of Christ's intercession and Word, as pictured in the laver. But when the Church passes from the scene of her earthly defilement into heaven, she will have no more need of the laver. The clear, ripple-free sea of glass in heaven declares that those in heaven are perfectly cleansed and at peace in God's presence. In heaven, God's people will no longer need to confess sin and obtain His cleansing – they will sin no more (1 Jn. 1:9).

Heavenly Creatures

John turns his attention from the seven flames of fire before God's throne to four spectacular creatures flying about it:

> *Before the throne there was a sea of glass, like crystal. And in the midst of the throne, and around the throne, were four living creatures full of eyes in front and in back. The first living creature was like a lion, the second living creature like a calf, the third living creature had a face like a man, and the fourth living creature was like a flying eagle. The four living creatures, each having six wings, were full of eyes around and within. And they do not rest day or night, saying: "Holy, holy, holy, Lord God Almighty, who was and is and is to come!"* (Rev. 4:6-8).

Besides this reference to the four living creatures, the Bible informs us that there are classes of spiritual beings that exist in heaven. Besides Michael the archangel, there are cherubim (Gen. 3:24; Ezek. 1:5-14;

10:7), seraphim (Isa. 6:1-7), the four living creatures just described, and a host of innumerable angels with various functions and roles (Ps. 103:19-22). Furthermore, God describes to us what many of these spiritual beings do and how they appear before God's throne in heaven. For example, the angel Gabriel announced the births of both the Lord Jesus and John the baptizer. The four living creatures and seraphim have the occupation of flying about God's throne and praising His name. All things recorded in Scripture have purpose, so why did God go to such effort to afford us these details? What is it that He wants us to learn?

It is my opinion that the Father is calling our attention to His Son through the appearance of these extraordinary heavenly creatures. That is, their intrinsic glories are concealed by their wings to ensure our attention remains focused on the Lamb of God, the Lord Jesus Christ. For example, the Seraphim have six wings, but only use two for flying (Isa. 6). The Cherubim were given four wings, but they also use only two for flying (Ezek. 1). God intended them to use their remaining wings to cover their own intrinsic glories while in His presence, thus assuring that only He would be adored and worshipped in heaven. Normally, these spiritual beings gladly cover themselves in God's presence, but there was a time when Lucifer, a special covering cherub, refused to cover himself and was lifted up in pride against God (Ezek. 28:13-16). He led a rebellion in heaven and likely took a third of the angels with him when he was cast out of God's presence (Isa. 14:12-15; Rev. 12:3-4, 9).

Returning to the spiritual creatures in heaven, we notice that not every part of these heavenly creatures is to be concealed with their wings; their feet, eyes, and faces are not to be covered in Revelation and, in fact, should not be, for some emulated glory of Christ is being proclaimed through their visibility. So what reflects Christ's glory is seen in these creatures, but what would compete with His glory is not described – we are not to be concerned with it. This exercise of revealing God's glory and concealing competing glories in God's presence is something that the Church is to remember and practice on earth; in so doing, we pattern the holy scene now occurring in heaven (1 Cor. 11:3-16). In fact, the angels learn about submission through this practice (1 Cor. 11:10).

The scriptural accounts of the cherubim in Ezekiel 1 and 10, of the seraphim in Isaiah 6, and of the four living creatures in Revelation 4 all disclose that these beings have four kinds of faces. Apparently, the cherubim each have all four, that is, the face of a lion, the face of an ox, the face of a man, and the face of an eagle. The faces of these beings reflect the same glories of the Lord Jesus that are presented in the main themes of each Gospel. The lion is the king of the beasts, which reflects Matthew's perspective of Christ as king. The ox, a beast of burden harnessed for the rigors of serving, pictures Mark's presentation of Jesus Christ, the servant. The face of the man clearly agrees with Luke's prevalent theme of the Lord's humanity. Lastly, the eagle flies high above all the other creatures – the divine essence of the Savior is in view here, as in the gospel of John. The many eyes of the cherubim describe Christ's omniscience and their bronze feet convey His divine authority to judge the wicked in flaming vengeance (Rev. 1:15). All that the Bible describes to us about heaven, whether in structures, furnishings, or angelic beings is for the purpose of calling our attention to God's Son!

God's Eternal City

The Bible begins and ends with a wedding. Both weddings occur in a beautiful garden and in the presence of God. In Genesis 2, the first wedding is of Adam and Eve in the Garden of Eden. The last wedding in the Bible is the marriage of the Lamb and His bride before the tree of life and at the very throne of God (Rev. 20-22). Because the New Jerusalem is full of redeemed people, an angel referred to the city as the Lamb's bride while speaking to John: *"'Come, I will show you the bride, the Lamb's wife.' And he carried me away in the Spirit to a great and high mountain, and showed me the great city, the holy Jerusalem, descending out of heaven from God"* (Rev. 21:9-10). Abraham knew about God's eternal city and was looking forward to seeing it (Heb. 11:10, 16). John saw this city and describes it for us:

> *He carried me away in the Spirit to a great and high mountain, and showed me the great city, the holy Jerusalem, descending out of heaven from God, having the glory of God. Her light was like a most precious stone, like a jasper stone, clear as crystal. Also she had a great and high wall with twelve gates, and twelve angels at the gates, and*

names written on them, which are the names of the twelve tribes of the children of Israel.... Now the wall of the city had twelve foundations, and on them were the names of the twelve apostles of the Lamb. ...The city is laid out as a square; its length is as great as its breadth ...twelve thousand furlongs. Its length, breadth, and height are equal. Then he measured its wall: one hundred and forty-four cubits, according to the measure of a man, that is, of an angel. The construction of its wall was of jasper; and the city was pure gold, like clear glass. The foundations of the wall of the city were adorned with all kinds of precious stones .... The twelve gates were twelve pearls: each individual gate was of one pearl. And the street of the city was pure gold, like transparent glass (Rev. 21:10-21).

I have visited some large cities, but this humongous heavenly city dwarfs them all. While all three dimensions of the city are 1500 miles, the height of its wall is nearly insignificant in comparison, only measuring 210 feet high (i.e., the city is 38,000 times higher than the wall encircling it). This would seem to indicate that protection of the city is not a concern, but rather the glory of it should be easily viewed by all. If viewable by those in hell, such a sight would certainly add to their agony of judgment.

The city has twelve foundations of precious stones and twelve pearl gates, but only one main street, and it is paved with gold. In this city, no matter how one enters it, all ways lead to the city's illuminating focal point – the throne of God: *"For the Lord God Almighty and the Lamb are its temple ... for the glory of God illuminated it. The Lamb is its light"* (Rev. 21:22-23). Although the sun and moon may exist in the eternal state, their light is not needed to illuminate the New Jerusalem. The Lord Jesus Christ will be its light!

God's Garden

John continues to describe the vista about God's throne: *"A pure river of water of life, clear as crystal, proceeding from the throne of God and of the Lamb. In the middle of its street, and on either side of the river, was the tree of life, which bore twelve fruits, each tree yielding its fruit every month"* (Rev. 22:1-2). Besides drinking from the pure river of water, the inhabitants of heaven are also invited to eat from the tree of life.

God calls our attention to three important trees in Scripture. The fruit from the tree of knowledge of good and evil was forbidden, but tasted by human desire (Gen. 3:1-7). The center of Scripture calls us to kneel before the suffering Savior nailed to a tree at Golgotha. Those who do are able to freely eat of the tree of life, which will be available in Heaven forever. The only remedy for sin and its handmaiden, death, is to obtain eternal life in Christ. Those who do will be able to eat freely from the tree of life.

After our first parents sinned, they were cast out of the Garden of Eden and prohibited from eating from the tree of life. Cherubim and a flaming sword guarded Eden to ensure every possible return route would be met with judgment – God prevented Adam and Eve from securing humanity's eternal doom. There is only one way to the tree of life: by Calvary's Road. The Lord Jesus declared, *"I am the way, the truth, and the life. No one comes to the Father except through Me"* (John 14:6). That is why there is only one street in heaven leading to the tree of life. The way to God was not man venturing in, but God coming out to man. The Son of God took the judgment of the flaming sword that we might have entrance to the tree of life.

Consequently, the Bible commences and ends with the Creator in fellowship with man in a garden paradise (Rev. 22:1-6). The journey man travels between these two gardens is a difficult one, but, thankfully, this journey is bridged by a third garden – *"Now in the place where He was crucified there was a garden; and in the garden a new sepulcher"* (John 19:41; KJV). Both the first Adam and the last Adam (Christ – 1 Cor. 15:45) died in a garden. The first Adam changed the first garden into a spiritual graveyard; the Lord Jesus rose from His garden tomb to offer spiritual life. Those who receive this provision will be restored to their Creator and be returned to an eternal garden paradise. Only through the center garden of Calvary may a connection between bliss and eternity be obtained.

Conclusion

The writer of Hebrews describes the inhabitants of God's eternal city: God, His Son, angels, Old Testament believers, the Church, and, in fact, all those redeemed by the blood of Christ (Heb. 12:22-24). John affirms that no human will be able to enter through any of New

Jerusalem's twelve gates unless their names are written in The Lamb's Book of life (Rev. 21:27). Dear reader, will you be able to enter into God's city and reside with Him forever? The Bible closes with this invitation: *"And let him who thirsts come. Whoever desires, let him take the water of life freely"* (Rev. 22:17). "Whoever will," my friend, means you; any one desiring to satisfy his or her deep yearning to be one with God is invited to come and drink of Him. *"Oh, taste and see that the Lord is good; blessed is the man who trusts in Him!"* (Ps. 34:8).

The Lord Jesus is the fullness and the fulfillment of the Old Testament covenants. *"For all the promises of God in Him are Yes, and in Him Amen, to the glory of God through us"* (2 Cor. 1:20). The Lord Jesus is the rightful heir to the throne of David and will deliver the Jews from all oppression, then rule over them in righteousness and peace forever. The Lord Jesus Christ is the hope of the Jewish nation of Israel. His coming to the air to rapture the Church from the earth prior to the Tribulation Period is the Church's blessed hope (1 Thess. 4:13-18; Titus 2:13). The hope of every believer is to be with the Lord Jesus and to have a glorified body that will serve and honor Him perfectly throughout eternity (1 Jn. 3:2-3). As the repentant thief who was crucified with the Lord soon discovered, wherever the Lord is – is paradise (Luke 23:43).

Heaven: Questions and Answers

1. Will there be individual time with the Lord in heaven?

From our space- and time-dependent perspective, it would seem that if there are millions of people in heaven, each person may not have access to the Lord. Certainly, much of the worship which will occur in heaven will be in unison with other believers and with various spiritual creatures (Rev. 5:11-14; 7:9-12). Yet, despite this fact, individuality among the throngs of heaven is not lost. Our need for individuality and personal recognition, however, will not be as it is now.

John tells us that every believer in heaven will be given a white stone with a special name written on it: *"And I will give him a white stone, and on the stone a new name written which no one knows except him who receives it"* (Rev. 2:17). This action indicates that although there will be many people in heaven, each person there will enjoy unique communion with Christ. The earthly trials that we face now mold our understanding and appreciation for the Savior – He means something a bit different to each of us. In life, we develop a unique appreciation for the Savior in ways that others cannot relate to specifically; this private admiration will be cherished throughout eternity. In fact, the Lord provides us with a stone with a special name on it which fits our understanding of Him. No one else will know that name but the recipient of the stone; this ensures that every believer will enjoy special intimacy with the Lord in a way that others cannot.

2. Will there be marriages and sexual relationships in heaven?

Contrary to the Mormon and Islamic views of heaven, people in heaven will neither be male nor female, at least not in the way we understand the genders to exist today. There will be no marriages or sexual relationships in heaven as these, and other world religions, claim. The Lord confirmed this truth while responding to a fictitious scenario posed by the Sadducees, a religious sect which formed part of the Jewish judicial court called the Sanhedrin. The Sadducees did not believe in the supernatural and thus mocked the doctrine of resurrection. They asked the Lord Jesus about a woman who had been married to seven different men (she was widowed seven times and never married to more than one man at once): *"In the resurrection, whose wife of the seven will she be? For they all had her"* (Matt. 22:28). Rather than preaching to them again a message they had already rejected, the Lord used the opportunity to affirm the truth of resurrection:

> *You are mistaken, not knowing the Scriptures nor the power of God. For in the resurrection they neither marry nor are given in marriage, but are like angels of God in heaven. But concerning the resurrection of the dead, have you not read what was spoken to you by God, saying, 'I am the God of Abraham, the God of Isaac, and the God of Jacob'? God is not the God of the dead, but of the living* (Matt. 22:29-32).

Those who experience resurrection will not be gender-significant. They will be like the angels, who are neither men nor women, although when they present themselves in human form to deliver God's messages, they have always appeared as men. For example, in Genesis 18, Abraham prepared a meal for three wayfaring men, who were later revealed to be the Lord and two of His angels.

Male and female genders were God's design to provide complementing companionship in marriage and for the purpose of procreation (Gen. 1:28; 2:18). In heaven, the need for reproduction will be eliminated – everyone will be eternal. Moreover, our communion with God in heaven will far exceed anything we could have ever experienced in an earthly relationship. Accordingly, we will be completely satisfied with being in fellowship with God and desire nothing else, including marital relationships. One of the clear warning signs of a false teaching is the notion that fleshly desires will be satisfied in heaven or, even worse, that such things are a part of some supreme deity's reward system.

We are three-part beings: spirit, soul, and body, and God wants to control all of us (1 Thess. 5:23). That goal will be achieved once believers have received their glorified bodies. In heaven, our human spirit (i.e., our inner man that is God-conscious) will perfectly control our soul (which composes our will, emotions, personality, and mental faculties) and our body. Our human spirit will be under the full control of the Holy Spirit, which will ensure deep satisfaction with God and that we will not covet any cheap substitutes at the flesh level.

3. What will we do in Heaven?

Unfortunately, many people have the impression that heaven will either consist of people sitting on puffy clouds while strumming their golden harps, or else engaging in the things they most enjoyed doing on earth. While the book of Revelation does mention that saints will sing and play harps, this is not for entertainment purposes; it is their contribution to the corporate worship of God (Rev. 5:8; 15:2). The redeemed will have the ability to sing and praise God with one voice. If you are hoping that there will be fishing, golfing, bowling, hunting, scrapbooking, knitting, etc. in heaven, I'm sorry to disappoint you, but there won't be. But be encouraged: if heaven is your final destination, you will not desire these activities anymore anyway.

Besides worshipping the Lord, the redeemed will rule and reign with Christ over the nations during His Millennial Kingdom on earth (2 Tim. 2:12; Rev. 4:4; 20:4). During this time, all the curses that were placed upon the earth as a result of human sin will be removed (Rom. 8:19-22). Those individuals who do not take the mark of the beast and live through the Tribulation Period will repopulate the earth during the Kingdom Age; the rest of the people on earth at Christ's Second Coming will be destroyed with the Antichrist and False Prophet (Matt. 25:31-41; Rev. 19:20-21). During this entire 1,000-year period, Satan and his angels will be confined to the bottomless pit (Rev. 20:1-3).

As mentioned previously, at the end of the Kingdom Age, Satan will be loosed from his prison and will attempt to deceive as many people as possible to rebel against the Lord. His goal will be to take as many people as possible to the Lake of Fire with him. Satan and the demons know their end (Luke 4:33-35; Matt. 25:41); their defeat certain, they content themselves with keeping people from worshipping God. At the Great White Throne judgment, all of the wicked, including the angels, will be judged by Christ. Believers will take part in that judgment process (1 Cor. 6:3). The believer has a bright future in Christ! Besides the opportunity to praise and worship the Lord with unhindered affections and unfailing strength, the believer also rules and reigns with Christ, judges the wicked with Christ, and inherits all things with Christ (Rev. 21:7). Being with Christ ensures that heaven will be a wonderful place to spend eternity.

4. Will we recognize others in heaven?

Martin Luther, the night before he died, was reasonably well and sat with his friends at a table. The matter of their discourse was whether or not we shall know one another in heaven. Luther held the affirmative position, and this was one reason he gave: Adam, as soon as he saw Eve, knew what she was, not by discourse, but by divine revelation; so shall we know others in the life to come.[1]

Scripturally speaking, the rich man suffering in Hades knew who Abraham and Lazarus were and who his brothers (still living) were. David said that he would see his deceased infant son again after death (2 Sam. 12:23). Those in Revelation who had been martyred during the Tribulation Period and had gone to heaven were fully cognizant of what had happened to them and requested that God take vengeance on their oppressors (Rev. 6:9-11). The disciples, though a bit confused at first, recognized the Lord Jesus after His resurrection (Luke 24:31; John 20:20).

Apparently, death does not prohibit us from recognizing loved ones, even if they have not yet experienced resurrection – we intuitively know their spiritual essence. There must, then, be the ability of individuals to distinguish other souls even when there is not a body; thus, it would stand to reason that individuals after experiencing resurrection would still be discernable (i.e., the resurrected body would contain the same soul that was recognized before). As explained earlier, the resurrected body draws characteristics from its mortal body (1 Cor. 15:37-39). This allows it to be similar in appearance to its previous earthly form. The resurrected body will represent God's best design for each individual; perhaps this is the reason that when angels appear in human form, they never appear as children or as elderly.

5. Will there be babies in heaven?

The short answer to this question is yes and no. I do not believe that we will see half-pint glorified people rollerblading down heaven's gold pavement. Each one there will be God's best impression of who he or she is and all will have the opportunity to see the Lord without requiring a stool or step-ladder. Nowhere in Scripture do we read of a heavenly nursery for departed babies or of children roaming about heaven. With that said, it is my opinion that those who die before understanding the moral law within them (Rom. 2:15), and God's solution for sin will be there in the same type of full-sized bodies that everyone else will have. These souls would not be part of the Church, but would nevertheless be trophies of God's grace.

In Adam, we all died (Rom. 5:12), so no matter how cute a baby is, he or she was born in sin (Ps. 51:5). This is why the Lord Jesus said, *"He who believes in Him is not condemned; but he who does not believe is condemned **already**, because he has not believed in the name of the only begotten Son of God"* (John 3:18). We all have been conceived and born into sin. Thus, a holy God would be just in condemning all rebels to the Lake of Fire; naturally speaking, we are all born as enemies of God (Rom. 5:6-10). But the Lord has a solution to this situation: *"But God, who is rich in mercy, because of His great love with which He loved us, even when we were dead in trespasses, made us alive together with Christ (by grace you have been saved)"* (Eph. 2:4-5). God can legitimately make such an offer because He judged His own Son for all of our sins – Christ took our place in death and judgment (Heb. 2:9). Those who accept this offer are *"not condemned,"* and those who reject it are *"condemned already"* (John 3:18).

God has a great concern for children, and threatens those who abuse them with dire consequences (Matt. 18:6). Children have guardian angels to provide a certain level of protection against the forces of evil which work to prevent them from understanding divine truth and turning to God (Matt. 18:10). Just as a shepherd with one hundred sheep is concerned about one lamb that strays from the fold, God is concerned about each child and desires that none be lost (Matt. 18:14).

But what about those people who have never had an opportunity to either accept or reject God's offer of salvation (i.e., embryos, newborns, the mentally disabled, etc.)? In other words, what about individuals who died before they were morally conscious and consequently did not hear of God's solution to their sin problem? There is not enough Scripture addressing this matter to make a conclusive statement, but the above conclusion (i.e., that these people will be granted a place in heaven) seems consistent with God's gracious character as demonstrated in similar situations. For example, those under twenty years of age were not judged with the older Israelites who had doubted and murmured against the Lord at Kadesh-barnea (Num. 14:29-33). As previously mentioned, David certainly believed that he would someday see his deceased newborn son in heaven (2 Sam. 12:23). There is one thing that we can be sure of in this matter: *"Shall not the Judge of all the earth do right?"* (Gen. 18:25). Yes, God will do what is right!

The Blessed Hope

The blessed hope of every Christian is the imminent appearance of the Lord Jesus Christ, at which time He will gather up the true Church from the earth to be with Him forever. This is the curtain call for the Church, the final call of all Christians. Glorification, the salvation of the body from the presence of sin, occurs at this moment for the Church. Each believer will receive an incorruptible, immortal, Christ-like body which cannot sin. In an instant, the flesh nature which was passed down from generation to generation will be completely eradicated once and for all. The indwelling sin which caused the believer so many difficulties on earth will be gone forever. This is Christ's total and final solution to sin. Until that time, John exhorts believers to serve with this living hope:

> *Beloved, now we are children of God; and it has not yet been revealed what we shall be, but we know that when He is revealed, we shall be like Him, for we shall see Him as He is. And everyone who has this hope in Him purifies himself, just as He is pure* (1 Jn. 3:2-3).

In heaven, believers will not struggle with fatigue, temptation, pride, envying, or inappropriate thoughts. Our unhindered attention and praise will be forever rendered to the One who delivered us from the penalty, power, and presence of sin. Eyes of faith, emboldened by Scripture, peer beyond this temporary realm of corruption to anticipate eternal bliss with Christ.

Get a Hope

The believer's hope is not in the salvation of the soul (that is received by trusting the gospel message). Rather, it is the salvation of the body at the Lord's coming (Rom. 13:11)! This is why Paul could say the conclusion of his salvation was closer than the day that he had first trusted Christ as Savior and was saved. What does the New Testament tell us about our hope in Christ?

The believer only has ONE HOPE (Eph. 4:4).

The BLESSED HOPE is Christ's appearing to receive His Church

    (1 Thess. 4:13-18; Titus 2:13).

There is REWARD for living out this HOPE (2 Tim. 4:8).

Those having this HOPE are prompted to live PURELY (1 Jn. 3:3).

Any rapture view other than the Pre-Tribulation position looks for the appearance of the Antichrist, not the coming of Lord Jesus Christ! There is a horrific period of upheaval called the Tribulation Period looming in the near future (Matt. 24:21). But as John acknowledged to the believers in the Church at Philadelphia, the Church will be brought home prior to this time of divine wrath: *"Because you have kept My command to persevere, I also will **keep you from** the hour of trial which shall come upon the whole world, to test those who dwell on the earth"* (Rev. 3:10). As mentioned previously, the Greek preposition *ek* is rightly translated "keep ... from" in this verse; if the Lord wished to signify that He would preserve the Church *through* the Tribulation, the Greek preposition *dia* would be required. The Lord will keep the Church out of the Tribulation Period, not preserve her through it. The Church will not experience God's wrath as He judges the wicked during the Tribulation Period (1 Thess. 1:10; 5:9). The entire Tribulation is a time of God's wrath. In fact, even the wicked are fully conscious that it is the Lamb, the Lord Jesus in heaven, who is judging them at this time (Rev. 6:15-17).

Stand for truth, dear believer! The Lord knows His own and He will sustain you until your service for Him is complete. Then you will enjoy His presence and watch Him judge those who resisted His truth. There is only one thing for believers to be concerned about at this present time: that we not pull back from living for Christ; those who do will experience shame at His appearing (1 Jn. 2:28).

Prophets of old, like Isaiah and Jeremiah, are good examples to follow: they stood fast in the face of great opposition and would not relent from speaking for God and conveying a message that, if heeded, would save lives. The fact that it was rejected by the majority did not discourage them from sharing it with others. The gospel message of Jesus Christ is vital to the salvation of millions of lost souls; may we also rejoice to share it as we wait expectantly for His imminent return. When we see our Beloved Savior, all that we hoped for, plus all that we could have never comprehended previously, will be ours in Christ forever.

Face to face with Christ, my Savior,
Face to face – what will it be?
When with rapture I behold Him,
Jesus Christ who died for me.

Only faintly now, I see Him,
With the darkling veil between,
But a blessed day is coming,
When His glory shall be seen.

What rejoicing in His presence,
When are banished grief and pain;
When the crooked ways are straightened,
And the dark things shall be plain.

Face to face! O blissful moment!
Face to face – to see and know;
Face to face with my Redeemer,
Jesus Christ who loves me so.

— Mrs. Frank A. Breck

Glossary

Abomination of Desolation: The Antichrist stops the Jewish sacrifices, desecrates the temple, and demands to be worshipped as God. This occurs just after the seventh trump judgment and is exactly 1260 days or 42 months or *"a time, times, and half a time"* (three and a half years) before Christ's return to destroy the Antichrist.

Adventism: In 1844, Christ entered the final stage of atoning ministry to judge and cleanse the redeemed in preparation of His second coming when saints will be taken to heaven for 1000 years and wickedness infests the world. All is destroyed at the end of the millennium.

Amillennialism: Good (the kingdom of God) and evil continue to grow in the world until Christ returns to the earth to defeat evil once and for all, thus beginning the eternal state. This view spiritualizes Christ's kingdom (i.e., there is no literal millennial reign of Christ on earth) and biblical promises to Israel.

Battle of Armageddon: At the end of the Tribulation Period, Jerusalem will be partially conquered when the Lord descends to engage the Antichrist in this battle. This conflict will occur in the Megiddo Valley where the armies of the world will have assembled against the Jewish nation. The Lord will completely obliterate them all with just an utterance from His mouth.

Beginning of Sorrows: An era marked by specific prophetic fulfillment which alerts the Jews to the forthcoming Tribulation Period. These troubling events are of an escalating nature and are signs to Israel.

Day of Christ: Refers to the rapture of the Church and the Judgment Seat of Christ where the value of the believer's work will be judged. The day of Christ is always spoken of in a positive light and is to be joyfully anticipated.

Day of God: Synonymous with the Eternal State – man enjoys eternal bliss with God without the presence of sin or evil.

Day of the Lord: An Old Testament term that speaks of those times when Jehovah intervened in a visible and powerful way to judge the wicked on earth. This meaning continues into the New Testament and speaks of the Tribulation Period and the millennial reign of Christ. The Day of the Lord concludes with the destruction of the earth and the subsequent Great White Throne judgment.

Eternal State: Synonymous with the Day of God and is the everlasting reality of a new heaven and new earth where man enjoys eternal bliss with God in paradise (the New Jerusalem) without the presence of sin or evil.

First Advent: The Son of God's incarnation to personally deliver God's message of peace to humanity some two thousand years ago. The Lord Jesus was both the message and the Messenger.

First Resurrection: Also referred to as the resurrection of life. This occurs for the righteous at several distinct points in time prior to the Great White Throne judgment. It is also called glorification because all believers receive a Christ-like immortal body which is the conclusion of God's work of salvation for those justified in Christ.

Fullness of the Gentiles: Marks the conclusion of the Church Age when the last believer is added to the body of Christ and is then raptured from the earth. The Church, which began at Pentecost, is predominately composed of Gentile believers.

Great Tribulation: Begins with the Abomination of Desolation and ends with the destruction of Antichrist.

Great White Throne Judgment: Where every knee will bow to the Lord Jesus Christ's authority and all those not justified in Christ will be eternally condemned.

Judgment Seat of Christ: Immediately follows the rapture of the Church from the earth and is where the value of each believer's work will be judged by Christ and eternal reward will be bestowed accordingly. This judgment is also related to the Day of Christ.

Judgment of the Nations: At Christ's Second Advent, He will punish all those who followed the Antichrist and persecuted the Jews during the Tribulation Period. This judgment is done suddenly and those unfit for Christ's kingdom will be abruptly removed from the earth.

Mid-Tribulation Rapture: This view states that the Church will be taken up after the seventh trumpet judgment which supposedly occurs at the midpoint in the Tribulation Period.

Partial Rapture: A position that states that only those believers "watching and waiting" for the Lord's coming will be raptured. This will happen at various times prior to and during the seven-year Tribulation Period.

Postmillennialism: Believers are diligently working to usher in Christ's kingdom on earth through gospel outreach efforts. Once the earth has been won for Christ and properly prepared, Christ will return to the earth; this event will be the culmination of the kingdom.

Post-Tribulation Rapture: This position asserts that living believers will not be raptured from the earth until Christ's Second Advent. The Church will be protected by God through the Tribulation Period and also will be further purified at that time.

Premillennialism: Christ will return to the earth at the end of the Tribulation Period to establish His righteous kingdom and reign on the earth for one thousand years.

Pre-Tribulation Rapture: Christ will return from heaven to the air to remove His Church from the earth before the seven-year Tribulation Period initiates.

Pre-Wrath Rapture: This position asserts that the Church will be raptured to heaven between the sixth and the seventh seal judgments and then the Day of the Lord will begin. The Church will endure the Great Tribulation but will be raptured to escape God's final judgments at the end of Daniel's seventh week.

Preterism: A literal-historical view that considers all major prophetic events to have been fulfilled in the first century (i.e., historical events from 66-70 AD are spiritualized). Accordingly, there is no rapture of the Church, no Tribulation Period, and no Millennial Kingdom to come. Some moderate Preterists believe in a literal second coming of Christ to the earth to establish a state of eternal bliss.

Rapture: Though not a biblical term, it describes the Greek verb *harpazo* which is translated "caught up" in 1 Thessalonians 4:17. It refers to the Church's being snatched from the earth with force to meet Christ in the clouds. This event occurs in a twinkling of an eye and believers will receive a glorified immortal body and return to heaven with the Lord.

Replacement Theology: A theological position that denies the Jews any opportunity for divine restoration as God's covenant people, a peaceful residence in the Promised Land, or a status of honor in Christ's future kingdom. This view claims that the Jews rejected their Messiah and therefore God is finished with them; hence, all God's covenant promises to the Jews have been fully transferred to those who would later be redeemed by Christ.

Second Advent: Christ's bodily and visible return to the earth to establish His glorious kingdom.

Second Death: Those not justified in Christ will be cast into the Lake of Fire (hell) to suffer eternal judgment.

Second Resurrection: All the condemned will be resurrected after Christ's Millennial Kingdom and be judged and condemned by the Lord Jesus Christ at the Great White Throne judgment.

Time of the Gentiles: A period of Gentile rule and oppression of the Jewish people that commenced with the destruction of Jerusalem by the Babylonians in 586 BC and will continue until the battle of Armageddon at the conclusion of the Tribulation Period.

Endnotes

Preface

Israel – The Apple of God's Eye
1. *Oxford English Dictionary* (Oxford University Press, NY); 1989
2. C. E. Hocking, *Rise Up My Love* (Precious Seed Publication, West Glamorgan, UK: 1988), p. 54
3. Corrie ten Boom, *Father ten Boom: God's Man* (Old Tappan, NJ: Fleming H. Revell, 1978), p. 67
4. Corrie ten Boom, with John and Elizabeth Sherrill, *The Hiding Place*, 25th Anniversary Ed. (Chosen Books, 1997; orig. Old Tappan, NJ: Fleming H. Revell, 1971), p. 68
5. George Lenczowski, *American Presidents and the Middle East* (Duke University Press, Durham, NC; 1990), p. 26
6. Norman Berdichevsky, "Israel: From Darling of the Left to Pariah State" (*New English Review*), May 2012

Allegories of Love

Grace and Faith from the Beginning
1. (Donald Barnhouse, *The Invisible War* (Zondervan Pub. House, Grand Rapids, MI; 1965), p. 107).

Seventy – Israel's Number
1. Sir Robert Anderson, *The Coming Prince;* Preface to the Tenth Edition http://www.WhatSaithTheScripture.com [last accessed March 28, 2017]
2. Ibid., chp. 5

Bible Prophecy in Motion
1. http://heavenawaits.wordpress.com/jewish-return-to-israel-in-end-times; 2010 and 2012 data calculated from latest Census information: *Monthly Bulletin of Statistics*. Israel Central Bureau of Statistics, March 7, 2013
2. Ynet, 2012-03-28, http://11tags.com/Israeli_Jews.html
3. www.jpost.com/NationalNews/Article.aspx?id=299548
4. Rabbi David E. Lipman, *The Birth of Israel,* http://www.myjewishlearning.com/israel/History/1948-1967/Birth_of_Israel.shtml
5. "Yemeni Jews Secretly Airlifted to Israel" (Jewishjournal.com), August 14, 2013
6. John Fedler, *Israeli Agriculture: Coping with Growth,* (JewishVirtualLibrary.org), 2007

Impending Predictions

1. http://data.worldbank.org/indicator/NY.GDP.MKTP.CD
2. Prophecy News, "Temple Institute Performs 'Educational, Passover Sacrifice" by Chris Perver; April 10, 2012, http://www.prophecynews.co.uk/index.php/temple-mount/1919-temple-institute-performs-educational-passover-sacrifice
3. F. F. Bruce, *Israel and the Nations* (Paternoster Press, UK; 1963), pp. 134-154

The Sign of the Unknown Tongue

Babylon Destroyed Forever

1. Herodotus Book 1: sections 178-186
2. Ibid., section 191
3. James B. Pritchard, *Ancient Near Eastern Texts Relating to the Old Testament* (Princeton University Press, Princeton, NJ; 1955), p. 306
4. David Down, *Investigator 17, 1991* (March): Reprinted courtesy of SIGNS OF THE TIMES 1983 Volume 98 Number 6).

The Exodus Connection

Jeremiah's "Beholds"

1. William Kelly, *Notes on Jeremiah and Lamentations*, http://www.stempublishing.com/authors/kelly/1Oldtest/jeremiah.html

Israel's Future in Review

God Is Not Done With Israel

Similar, but Different

1. Renald E. Showers, *There Really is a Difference! A Comparison of Covenant and Dispensational Theology* (The Friends of Israel Gospel Ministry, Inc: Bellmawr, NJ, 1990)
2. Charles C. Ryrie, *Dispensationalism, Revised and Expanded* (Moody Press: Chicago, IL; 1995), pp. 183-184

What Is the Church's Hope?

Two Resurrections

Millennial Views

1. Mark Hitchcock, *The End Times Controversy: The Stake in the Heart – AD 95 Date of Revelation* (Harvest House, Eugene, OR; 2003), p. 150.
2. Ellen White, *The Great Controversy* (1858, Chp. 16)

Endnotes

Rapture Views

A Body Fit for Heaven
1. P. L. Tan, *Encyclopedia of 7700 illustrations* (Bible Communications, Garland TX; 1996, c1979); #2195

What Will Heaven Be Like?
1. P. L. Tan, op. cit., 2197
2. Jim Flanigan, *Notes on Revelation* (Gospel Tract Publications; 1987), pp. 40-41
3. William Kelly, *The Elders in Heaven*,
    http://www.stempublishing.com/authors/kelly/7subjcts/eldershv.html

Heaven: Questions and Answers
1. P. L. Tan, op. cit., 2196

The Blessed Hope

Glossary

www.ingramcontent.com/pod-product-compliance
Lightning Source LLC
La Vergne TN
LVHW051628080426
835511LV00016B/2229